the BLACK COAST

the BLACK COAST

the story of the PT boat by BASIL HEATTER

Farrar, Straus and Giroux • *New York* •

This book is dedicated to all who were there

FOREWORD

~~~~~~

▼

The two boats lay a quarter of a mile off the shore. It was midnight, December 1943, on the black coast of New Guinea. There were no lights to be seen along the coast; indeed, because of the war, there were no lights for a thousand miles in any direction. The boats lay quietly with their noses pointed toward the beach. On the bow of each boat was painted a shark's jaw with great white teeth. In the dark no one could see the shark jaws, but the crews of the boats knew they were there and somehow felt better because of it.

From behind each patrol-torpedo boat came the mutter of underwater exhausts. The sound was like the low growling of four hundred hungry lions. Each boat was eighty feet long and had three 1500-horsepower engines. When all three engines were opened up, they had enough power to drive the boats clear of the water. When 80 tons of boat hit the water again at 40 knots, the impact could drive a man's leg bones through his skin.

The air tasted of salt and smelled of flowers. The salt was of the sea and the flowers were of the land, the ripe, rotting jungle only a few hundred yards away. Someone on one of the boats coughed nervously. Someone else hissed at him to be quiet. The man who had coughed had a strange taste in his mouth, a taste of brass and dust. What he was tasting was his own fear. Once the shooting started, he would be all right. He always was. But in this period of waiting his mouth had that strange, brassy taste.

The skippers of the two boats stood behind their wheels searching the blackness. There was nothing to be seen— the sea, the sky, and the horizon in between were almost equally black. Except for the smell of the land, they would not have known it was there. Now and then their eyes strayed to the dials of the instrument panels, lit by black light with a weird greenish glow like undersea creatures a thousand fathoms below the surface. One of the skipper's hands was on the engine indicators, and the other was spread across three red-knobbed throttles. When those three knobs were thrown forward and 4500 horse-power went suddenly to work, the PT boat would stand on its tail like a startled cat.

What they were waiting for was the moon. When the moon came up, it would enable them to see the coast and the enemy moving along it. It would also enable the enemy to see them. When that happened, the orange balls of tracer fire would come sailing out at them like long outfield flies. The orange balls always seemed to move with deceptive slowness and looked harmless; that is, until they went by with the rush and roar of express trains.

The gunners waited, the boats waited; the night held its breath. Behind them, a silver glow started in the sky. A beautiful moon, a bomber's moon, a PT boater's moon. By its soft glow the skipper of the lead boat could see something moving. It was big and black and had a white bone in its teeth. Although he could not see it clearly, he knew that it was a Japanese armored barge. The skipper felt a tickling in his stomach, a tingling in his palms. "Here we go," he called, and thrust the throttles home. At that moment something big and orange, like a second smaller moon, came sailing out toward him. The skipper spun the wheel hard over, the engines screamed, and as the boat fell over on its beam ends, spray washed across the deck and, behind them, the pretty orange balloon blew an immense red hole in the ocean.

It was now one minute after twelve. The start of a new day, the end of an old one, the middle of a PT boater's moonlit night.

This is the story of how they got there and what they did and what became of them.

the BLACK COAST

1

Warships are born, not made. They are born out of the necessity of the time and available skills and materials. The Greek trireme with its great bronze ram and massed banks of oarsmen was as up to date at the moment of its conception as a modern guided-missile cruiser is today. Nelson's *Victory* and our own *Old Ironsides* were the last word in the full-rigged fighting ships of the day. The aircraft carrier was born of the necessity for a flat-decked ship capable of landing aircraft. The PT boat was born of the need for a small, fast, inexpensive warship that could be mass-produced.

The first torpedo boat was built in England in 1905 by a boatbuilder named Yarrow. This first boat was only fifteen feet long and was powered by a single Italian Napier engine. It carried two small torpedoes and managed to turn up the then quite remarkable speed of 25 knots.

In the same year, another British builder, Thornycroft, produced a considerably larger boat—forty feet overall —with a top speed of 18 knots. Not bad at all for a boat weighing four and a half tons. It was the Thornycroft that pretty much set the style for the boats that were to follow.

In 1906 the Italians came up with a motor torpedo boat, and a year later the French also demonstrated a steel-hulled boat with a single torpedo tube built into the bow. Knowing what engines were like in those days, it is hard to imagine how such a boat could even have gotten out of its own way, but apparently it did, because the French were so much encouraged by its sea trials that they immediately ordered further development of it. Only in the United States, among the great sea powers of the time, was there little interest in the development of torpedo boats. The reason is not hard to find. Our geographical isolation from Europe made it highly unlikely that an enemy fleet could harass our coasts. Navy planners thought principally in terms of long-range engagements, probably fought thousands of miles away, in which small, high-speed boats would have been of little use.

Torpedo boats were being built in the United States, however, but not for our own use. In 1908, three years after the first Thornycroft boat had been built in England, an American boatbuilder named Nixon came up with a clever design for a torpedo boat which he sold to the Russians. These boats were twin-engined and propelled not by gasoline engines but by six-cylinder benzine engines. Benzine is even more explosive than gasoline, and it was a wonder the boats did not blow up before ever putting to sea. But apparently Nixon was either a genius at design or monumentally lucky because he got his ten boats to Russia. One of them even managed to cross from New York to Sevastopol under its own power, which would be considered a pretty remarkable stunt even today.

The first motor torpedo boats to go into combat were those of the Italians. The Italian Navy, which has not especially distinguished itself in other respects, has always had something of a flare for unorthodox boats such as the one-man submarine or the small, high-speed torpedo boat. As we know from their later production of sports cars, the Italians could build first-rate high-speed engines, and by 1916—the middle of World War I—the Italians had a considerable fleet of boats operating against the Austrian naval units in the Adriatic. These boats distinguished themselves by being the first torpedo boats ever to sink an enemy capital ship. On December 8, 1917, an Italian MAS boat sank the light cruiser *Wien* at Trieste, and six months later another flock of MAS boats sent the battleship *Svent Istvan* to the bottom in the Straits of Otranto.

The sinking of the *Svent Istvan* by the tiny Italian mosquito boats was roughly comparable to David's destruction of Goliath with a pebble hurled from a slingshot. The introduction of radar and automatic fire control in World War II made such a performance by torpedo boats almost impossible. In time, to meet the changing requirements, they became more gunboats than torpedo boats.

At the same time that the Italian MAS boats were performing such prodigies against the Austrians, the British motor torpedo boats were having almost equal success against the Germans in the English Channel and along the

5

coast of northern Europe. These boats, called CMB's (coastal motor boats), were a further improvement on the original Thornycroft design. They were hardly more than big floating torpedo tubes. Thirty feet long and not much more than three feet wide, they had no seats or other accommodations. The single torpedo was mounted in a tube that ran the length of the hull and was armed by the turning of a hand crank. The operation was particularly dangerous because, after the torpedo was dropped out of the tube astern of the boat, the boat had to get out of the way or it would be blown up by its own "fish." If the torpedo did not quite clear the tube, though already armed and running, the boat's life span could be measured in terms of seconds. The crews of these boats were the original "expendables." Their devil-may-care attitudes and odd "uniforms"—ragged pants and shirts, or no shirts at all—made them famous throughout the Allied navies.

A measure of the success of these boats was that by the time the war ended in 1918 the Royal Navy had commissioned sixty-six CBM's and was well along with plans for a seventy-footer, which would have been put into production if the war had continued. The boats were not so successful against air attack. On August 10, 1918, eight German fighter planes strafed six CMB's and put them all out of action. Despite their maneuverability, the CMB's simply did not carry enough guns to cope with low-flying planes. Even twenty-five years later, when American PT's carried more guns for their size than any other ship afloat, they still did their best to avoid daylight engagements with Japanese aircraft.

Surprisingly, the CMB's had their greatest success after the war. At that time, in 1919, the Allies were attempting to put down the Russian Revolution, and CMB's were used in a raid on the great Russian naval base at Kronstadt. The CMB's managed to slip inside the harbor defenses and sink the cruiser *Oleg,* at the same time disabling two more capital ships and two destroyers. All this with the loss of only one CMB.

Thus, as the war in Europe drew to a close, the torpedo boats had more than proved their worth. By 1920, even the American Navy was beginning to run tests on the small, high-speed boats that carried such a potent sting in their tails.

Strangely enough, the major contributions to the performance of high-speed motor boats in the years between the two great wars were made by a group of seagoing smugglers known as rumrunners. The Prohibition law had been passed in the United States making it illegal to sell liquor. As a result, the American people developed a thirst of overwhelming proportions. It was partly slaked by the activities of whiskey smugglers, who ran their cargoes ashore in the dead of night from outside the three-mile limit.

The boats that were used for this purpose not only had to be faster than the Coast Guard boats that would pursue them, but also had to be able to travel at high speeds in rough seas. Great amounts of liquor were smuggled ashore on the coast of Florida after a crossing from the British islands of the Bahamas. While the distance across the Gulf Stream between Bimini and Miami is not more than fifty miles, it can be fifty of the roughest sea miles in the world. And at the end of the voyage it was necessary to outrun the prowling Coast Guardsmen. It was a considerable boat indeed that could carry a substantial payload and still meet all these requirements. The boat, in short, would have to meet, basically, the requirements of a PT boat. Many of the lessons learned by the rumrunners about high-speed hulls and engines were put to good use by the Navy as World War II loomed on the horizon.

The next designer after Thornycroft to make an impact on PT design was another Englishman, Hubert Scott-Paine. In 1934, Scott-Paine completed plans for a sixty-foot torpedo boat which might be considered the forerunner of the American PT. Six of these boats were sold to the British Admiralty and demonstrated their sea-keeping ability by crossing all the way from England to Malta under their own power.

In 1939, as the shadow of World War II lengthened across Europe, Scott-Paine completed a somewhat larger torpedo boat. This one was seventy feet long and could carry two torpedoes twenty-one inches in width, or four torpedoes eighteen inches in width. In addition, it mounted a power-driven machine-gun turret on each side of the cockpit. This boat underwent sea trials on June 15, 1939, crossing the English Channel and returning against a moderate chop at an average speed of 42 knots. The Royal Navy was delighted with the results and placed an order for fifty of these larger and faster boats.

This purchase by the Royal Navy of what was then acknowledged to be the best torpedo boat yet produced created something of a stir in Washington naval circles, but still no large scale appropriation was forthcoming for the development of PT boats. What the Navy did do, however, was to announce a design contest for small, high-speed craft, with a prize of $15,000 for the winner in each class. In view of the world situation at the time,

8

it would have saved a considerable amount of money and a great deal of effort if the Navy had been willing to profit by the development of the then almost perfected Scott-Paine boat, but it did not.

Twenty-four designs were submitted and two were finally selected for further development. The delays, at a time when Hitler and Hirohito were shaking their fists in our direction, might have gone on for years, had it not been for the initiative of a private citizen named Henry R. Sutphen. Sutphen was the head of the Electric Boat Company, which had already built a good number of submarines for the Navy. Mr. Sutphen was convinced that the American Navy would soon be in urgent need of torpedo boats, and he determined to cut through the red tape by going to England on his own and purchasing, as a private citizen, one of the new Scott-Paine boats. He brought the boat back with him as deck cargo on board the SS *President Roosevelt*. The boat arrived in New York on September 5, 1939. This was clearly the turning point of the American torpedo-boat development. For it was from that boat that all the hundreds of future American PT's were to be born. World War II had started in Europe just two days earlier.

With all of this, however, it was not until June 17, 1940, that the first boat built by Elco (Electric Boat Company) was finally completed and delivered. She was called PT 9. The United States Navy had its first PT boat.

A number of boats were built from this Scott-Paine design (many of them were later transferred back to the British under Lend Lease), but the Navy was still not satisfied that it had achieved the ultimate in torpedo-boat design. Accordingly, in late July 1941, seven different types

9

of boats by different manufacturers were tested in a series of competitions that came to be known as the "Plywood Derby."

The single most important event of the contest was a run at full throttle for a distance of 190 miles in the open ocean off the eastern tip of Long Island. In that run the Elco seventy-seven-footers, a somewhat enlarged version of the original Scott-Paine design, clearly demonstrated their superiority at an average speed of close to 40 knots. Thus, although other manufacturers (Huckins and Higgins, principally) built several squadrons of PT boats, it was the eighty-foot Elco and the seventy-eight-foot Higgins that became the workhorses of America's growing PT-boat fleet.

With construction at last underway, it became necessary to create a training program for crew and officers who would man the boats. The Motor Torpedo Boat Squadrons Training Center was established at Melville, Rhode Island, a choice of site which will probably always remain a mystery to the men who received their training there. Situated on the shore of Narragansett Bay, the base was often frozen in during the winter months, making PT-boat operations impossible. When the base was not surrounded by ice, it was often so deep in mud that student officers felt it a considerable victory simply to navigate from one Quonset hut to another.

Possibly it was felt that if the students could survive the rigors of the school, they would find the hardships of combat bearable. Or possibly the purpose was simply to separate the "men from the boys." From that standpoint the school was probably successful. One of the "boys" who went in and came out a "man" was a gangling young ensign from Boston named John F. Kennedy. With the rest of his class, he went through the ordeal of Melville and moved on out to the Pacific, where his PT 109 was to become world famous. At the time, of course, no one at Melville had any way of knowing that young Mr. Kennedy had been earmarked by destiny as a President of the United States. He was simply another young officer who underwent the rigorous training period.

•

At the time of the Japanese attack on Pearl Harbor, few Americans understood the events that had led up to the declaration of war. In fact, few Americans at the time even knew where Pearl Harbor was. Although there had been talk of a possible war with Japan for many months, and even years, before the attack, hardly anyone really believed it would come. It was popular in those days to tell oneself that Japan did not have enough oil to fight a war, that all Japanese were bandy-legged little men whose eyesight was so defective that they could not possibly aim modern weapons or man modern ships or fly modern planes.

What, then, was the truth? Who were the Japanese, and what did they have against the United States? We thought of them as people of a feudal society who, before the arrival of an American admiral, had never been exposed to Western civilization. How could such a nation even dream of war against the American might? And even if they did dream of it, nothing could come of it. We were assured by our military experts that in the event of war we could crush the Japanese within two weeks.

It took four years. And it took not only PT boats and

every other type of naval vessel, but nuclear weapons as well.

We now know from captured documents that the Japanese attack on our fleet had been planned for many years. The Japanese had been secretly holding war maneuvers and had begun construction of the mightiest warships the world had ever seen—the *Yamato* and the *Musashi*—battleships so large they staggered the imagination. These ships had a displacement of 68,000 tons. The largest of our own modern battleships were in the *Iowa* class, with a displacement of 45,000 tons.

Why did the Japanese want war with us? To put it very simply, they were as dedicated to conquest in the East as Hitler was in the West. *Hakko Ichiu*—which means "bringing the eight corners of the world under one roof" —became the national slogan of Japan. If they could not rule the entire world, they would rule at least half of the eight corners—the half that lay in Asia. There was nothing to stop them but the American fleet, and they knew exactly what they would do about that.

So powerful were Japan's military leaders that any civilian, up to and including the premier, was in danger of assassination if he attempted to oppose them. Every Japanese was ambitious to serve in the armed forces and happy to die for the emperor. It was his belief that anyone who died fighting for the emperor would go straight to heaven and become one of the demigods protecting the Imperial homeland.

In 1931 the Japanese Army had invaded Manchuria at the instigation of the notorious Black Dragon, a secret society that had been advocating war with China for many years. But the war did not go as well as the Army had hoped; it was time for the Navy to have a chance.

The rise of the Japanese Navy is a modern phenomenon. In 1922 it had only half the combat tonnage of either the American or the British fleets. By 1941 it had a stronger force in the Pacific than both these navies put together. In addition, it had better torpedoes, better optical equipment, and bigger guns. It did not have oil, but it planned to take that by conquest.

In May 1941—six months before the Japanese attacked —the relative strength of the American and Japanese navies in the Pacific was as follows: America had nine battleships, against ten for the Japanese; three carriers, against ten of theirs; twelve heavy cruisers, against eighteen Japanese cruisers; nine American light cruisers against seventeen Japanese; sixty-seven American destroyers, against a hundred and eleven Japanese; and twenty-seven submarines, against sixty-four Japanese.

In 1941 the Japanese Navy was the best in the world, or at least in their part of the world. And still most Americans did not know where Pearl Harbor was. Fortunately, there were some, like Henry Sutphen, who foresaw the day when America would need every ship and plane she could muster. It took years to build a battleship or a carrier, and America did not have years. The obvious answer then was a ship that could be built quickly and inexpensively and still pack a wallop. The PT boat was part of the answer to *Hakko Ichiu*.

2

▼

By the morning of December 7, 1941, when the Japanese planes appeared off Diamond Head in their devastating sneak attack on the United States Navy at Pearl Harbor, there were three squadrons of PT's in the Navy. Two of these were on active duty in the Pacific.

MTB (Motor Torpedo Boat) Squadron 1 had twelve boats at Pearl Harbor, and MTB Squadron 3 had six boats, under the command of Lieutenant John D. Bulkley, at Manila Bay in the Philippines. It took the Japanese four months to crush the stubborn defenders of Corregidor, and during that time Squadron 3 was almost the only active Naval force engaging the enemy in the Philippines.

The first shots fired in anger by American PT boats came early on the morning of December 7 at Pearl Harbor. Six PT's of Squadron 1 were moored alongside the submarine base. It was a peaceful, sunny morning and those men and officers who were not ashore were enjoying a leisurely Sunday breakfast. Sunday was not a working day in the peacetime Navy, and, in that bright sunshine, certainly the last thing on the men's minds was the threat of war. Imagine their astonishment when they heard the thunder of the first bombs dropping along Battleship Row.

They responded promptly. Within a matter of seconds, the twin-mounted .50 caliber machine guns of PT 23 were hurling lead into the sky. For men who could not yet realize that there was a war on, their marksmanship was remarkably good. They downed a low-flying Japanese torpedo plane over the tip of Kuahua Island and brought down another over Magazine Point near the submarine base. Thus, to PT 23 goes the honor of drawing first blood in the grim struggle that was to last four years.

And what of the six boats that were at Cavite Navy Yard on the shore of Manila Bay? The Japanese heavy air strike on Manila came on December 10, three days after the attack on Pearl Harbor. The ships and planes concentrated around Manila might have been dispersed to less vulnerable positions during those three days, but they were not. It hardly matters now who was to blame for this error, but the sad fact remains that American forces in the Philippines were caught by surprise almost as much as those at Pearl Harbor.

The attack on the Navy Yard began at 1:14 on the afternoon of December 10 and continued until almost 2:30. During that time the boats of Squadron 3 zigzagged back and forth, guns blazing. Three waves of twenty-seven bombers each swept over the city, destroying the entire Navy Yard and almost half of the city of Cavite.

One fact had been established by the raid; PT boats could outmaneuver dive bombers in daylight. Provided the PT skipper was cool enough to hold his course until the bombs had actually left the plane's bomb bay, he could then hurl his boat over into a 180-degree turn to either side, which was usually enough to put the falling bombs abeam or astern. Obviously, this maneuver called for iron nerves on the part of the skipper and his crew, but iron nerves were not at a premium in those early days of the war. What had been only theory until then became accepted practice and was proved many times over in the next four years.

The PT's distinguished themselves that day at Cavite by shooting down at least three dive bombers. After that, the incoming planes gave the PT's a wide berth, concentrating on less nimble, less ferocious targets. The chief of staff later sent Lieutenant Bulkley a message in which he said: "The latest report is that three dive bombers were seen being chased over Marivales Mountain by an MTB. Don't you think this is carrying the war a bit too far?"

Squadron 3 was ready to carry the war right to Tokyo if need be, but it was severely handicapped by the loss of all its stores and spare parts in the destruction of the Navy Yard. PT's, like all high-speed craft, are comparatively fragile and require constant attention. Now, with their spare engines and high-test gasoline gone, the boats of Squadron 3 soon began to feel the pinch.

On the night of January 18, Bulkley received a report of four enemy ships lying off Binanga Bay. The force was said to include one destroyer and one large transport. Two PT boats were ordered to attack.

The two boats, 31 and 34, separated at the mouth of Subic Bay shortly after midnight, and 34 crept in toward the enemy, which could scarcely be seen as a darker blur against the sky. The PT had not gone very far before it was challenged by a light and then a heavy burst of machine-gun fire. PT 34 responded by firing two torpedoes at the nearest target, a two-masted freighter. One of the torpedoes struck the Japanese ship, but the other fish never left the PT; it stuck in the tube in what was called a "hot run."

There are few experiences more uncomfortable for a PT sailor than a hot run on deck. This means that although the torpedo is stuck in the tube its propellers are turning. Without water resistance, the propellers turn faster and faster until finally the torpedo casing and all its innards are blown apart, spreading white-hot shrapnel across the boat. The only way to prevent the explosion is to straddle the tube and turn off the air-line valve to the combustion pot. In theory it doesn't sound too difficult, but in practice it is a little like waltzing with an enraged tiger. A ton of roaring, hissing torpedo that may go off in your face at any moment is not the pleasantest of playmates at midnight on the heaving deck of a PT.

John Martino, the chief torpedoman of the 34, was equal to the occasion. He secured the air valve and was able to stop the hot run, but the danger was not over. The fish was still half in and half out of the tube and every time the bow of the boat dipped into the water the torpedo impeller blades were turned. After the proper number of turns, the torpedo would again be armed and ready to explode. Once again Martino straddled the hissing monster, this time leaning far out over the water to stuff a wad of toilet paper into the blades to keep them from turning.

This was only the first of many torpedo problems encountered by the boats. Often the skipper of a boat might make a perfect run on target and launch his fish, only to see it either sink, or porpoise into the air. Occasionally one of the erratic fish even chased its own boat. Later in the war, this situation was improved somewhat by the introduction of aircraft torpedoes instead of the standard destroyer torpedoes, but this brought on a new set of problems because there were no tubes to fit these fatter torpedoes. They had to be installed on deck in improvised racks and simply rolled over the side like depth charges. It was hardly the ideal way to launch so delicate a mechanism as a torpedo.

In any event, bad torpedoes or not, PT 34 did manage to score a hit on a freighter that night and returned safely to base. But all did not go as well with PT 31, which was suffering from a lack of spare strainers and the clogging effects of poor gasoline. With its engines inoperative, the 31 drifted onto a reef and had to be blown up by its crew. This was done by chopping holes in the gasoline tanks and then tossing in a hand grenade, a method that became standard operating procedure for boats that could not be salvaged. Like stuffing toilet paper into the spinning impeller blades, this was not a method that was mentioned in any of the manuals.

Even though the war was only a few weeks old, the PT skippers were already finding out that combat conditions called for improvisations. Back at the PT training center in Melville, instruction still included the complicated formations by which fleets of naval craft, since the days of World War I at Scapa Flow, had attacked other naval craft. These were the classic maneuvers known as Crossing the Tee and Vee of Vees. Conceivably, battleships and cruisers might still use these maneuvers, but to expect PT's to use them was a little like teaching the lessons of Waterloo to a gang of Comanches.

The MTB's were in truth the Red Indians of naval warfare. When they attacked their larger targets, it was with the same methods the Indians employed against slow-moving wagon trains. Around and around went the high-speed boats in clouds of spray and with all guns blazing. Under those conditions, none of the classic maneuvers so painstakingly taught at the training center were worth a hoot. But this had to be learned and unlearned the hard way in the grim months and years that followed Squadron 3's first contact with the enemy in the Philippines.

But by the end of February, the defense of Corregidor against the superior Japanese forces was drawing to a close, and MTB Squadron 3 was down to its last two boats. It was at that point that General Douglas MacArthur, commanding the American forces in the Philippines, was ordered to withdraw to Australia and the PT's were given the job of evacuating the general and his family. The PT's successfully carried out their part of the mission, and when Lieutenant Bulkley returned to the United States, he was awarded the Medal of Honor—the nation's highest award for gallantry in combat—by President Franklin Delano Roosevelt.

General MacArthur was so enthusiastic about the performance of the PT boats that he sent a message to the President asking that PT's be established as a separate branch of the service and that two-hundred PT's be dis-

20

patched to the waters around the Philippines within the next eight months.

The general was somewhat optimistic in his estimate. It took four years to bring two hundred PT's to the Pacific, and the way was long and hard.

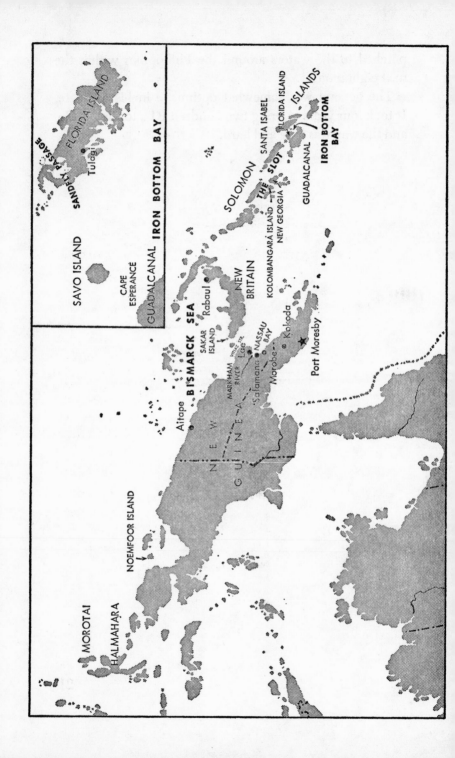

3

▼

After the rumble of exhaust of the last PT boat in the Philippines had died away, six long months were to go by before the motor torpedo boats were again active in the Pacific. This time it was to play a major role in what was perhaps the most grueling military campaign ever fought by American forces—Guadalcanal.

For more than half a year after the shock of Pearl Harbor, the Japanese had their own way in the Pacific. The great British naval base at Singapore had fallen and two of the Royal Navy's best ships—*Repulse* and *Prince of Wales*—had been sunk by Japanese aircraft. It began to seem as though nothing could stop or even delay the Japanese tide of conquest. But finally, on August 7, 1942, although we had still not recovered from the terrible losses inflicted on our Navy at Pearl Harbor, we took the offensive. It came with the landing of the First Marine Division on Guadalcanal.

We often dream of beautiful tropic islands in the Pacific. And some islands, like Tahiti and Samoa, are beautiful. Even the Solomons with their necklace of reefs and creamy surf are beautiful from a distance. When in the sixteenth century the Portuguese explorer Alvaro Mendaña, sailing west from Peru, first saw the Solomons, he thought them the most beautiful islands he had ever seen, and he named the largest Santa Isabel, in honor of the saint who had protected him on the long voyage.

But when that first explorer landed, he found that his dream of a lovely tropical island had turned into a nightmare. The natives were cannibals and headhunters (to this day a man can still lose his head in the Solomons), and the islands were alive with poisonous snakes, giant rats, and great ugly frogs as big as a man's head. The rotting jungle also bred every imaginable kind of fever and sickness. Even four hundred years later, when the American writer Jack London came to the Solomons, he wrote: "If I were a king the worst punishment I could inflict on my enemies would be to banish them to the Solomons. On second thought, king or no king, I don't think I'd have the heart to do it." This was the region chosen for the United States to make its first real stand against the Japanese. It was to prove the turning point of the war.

The First Marine Division was landed on Guadalcanal on August 7. In the months that followed, the Marines clung to their beachhead and slowly enlarged it against stiffening Japanese resistance. Fierce battles were fought for the possession of Henderson Field—the island's only airstrip—and for control of the sea lanes to the Solomons. At one point it looked as though the Navy would be forced to withdraw altogether, leaving the Marines to fend for themselves without supplies or support of any kind.

The low point came when, in a matter of a few hours one night, three American and one Australian cruiser were sunk by the Japanese off Savo Island. The bodies of hundreds of sailors were washed ashore next morning. Indeed, so many ships were sunk in the weeks and months that followed that the area surrounding the island came to be called Iron Bottom Bay. There was hardly a foot of it which did not contain a sunken ship. This was the situation on the night of October 11 when the first PT boats of the rebuilt Squadron 3 approached Guadalcanal.

As if the PT's had brought good luck with them, the tide began to turn on the very night of their arrival. The Japanese had determined once and for all to destroy Henderson Field. Without land-based planes to cover them, our forces ashore would be finished. In a smashing victory that came to be known as the Battle of Cape Esperance, the Japanese task force was turned back, but not without heavy losses on our side as well. The destroyer *Duncan* was sunk, and the cruisers *Boise* and *Salt Lake City* were badly damaged. But for the moment the Japanese were halted.

Two nights later, however, the Japanese returned in force. And that was when the PT's went into action. Imagine these tiny boats leaving the shelter of their base to feel their way out into the inky blackness of unmarked waters they had never seen before. Not only was the enemy ahead, but there were also coral reefs that could rip out the wooden bottoms of the boats, leaving the crew to be devoured by the giant sharks that roamed the waters between Tulagi and Guadalcanal.

Ahead is nothing but blackness. At the helm of each boat, the skipper alternately watches his dials to see that his engines are functioning properly and tries to distinguish the phosphorescent wake of the boat ahead to judge his distance. On the horizon, they suddenly see the tremendous orange flashes of the naval guns. A large-scale battle is in progress. At a signal from the lead boat, they increase speed. Suddenly a shaft of white light from the searchlight of an enemy destroyer sweeps over the lead boat. For a moment the boat is held in the light like a bug on the end of a pin. The men see each other's strained, pale faces in that intense, blue-white light, and then the PT swerves aside into the cover of darkness again.

That moment of illumination is for them like the so-called moment of truth in the bullring. They know now that the enemy is no longer a distant glow on the horizon; he is all around them in the dark.

Lieutenant Searles, at the wheel of PT 38, can barely make out the outline of what looks like an apartment house off to the right. He knows very well there are no apartment houses in the Solomons. He peers into the blackness, and now he can make out masts and the outlines of gun turrets—possibly a battleship, at the very least a light cruiser. He turns slowly toward the target. The range is closing. With a finger that is none too steady, he reaches forward and touches the button that controls the torpedo firing device. There is a hollow thud as the shotgun-shell detonator explodes and then a woosh of air as the great oily body of the torpedo leaves its tube. Immediately he fires another fish from the port tube and then almost simultaneously fires his two after-fish. Then he gives his boat full throttle.

Free of the four tons of dead weight imposed on it by the torpedoes, the boat leaps ahead. Again searchlights probe out of the blackness. Lieutenant Searles wrenches the wheel hard over, and the PT, darting between the searchlight beams, swings astern of the cruiser. At the same moment there is a great blast of heat and light just forward of the cruiser's bridge. It is followed almost immediately by another explosion. At least one and possibly two of the 38 boat's fish have struck home. The PT's have entered the battle for Guadalcanal.

Someone claps Searles on the back and shouts, "We got him, Skipper!"

With the cruiser blazing behind her, the PT vanishes into the darkness.

Meanwhile, the 60 boat is caught in the searchlights of two destroyers. They are after her like dogs after a fox. She turns and twists, doubling back in her own tracks, but the lights follow wherever she goes. Now the destroyers have opened fire, and the first shell lands only twenty feet astern. The explosion lifts the boat right out of the water, but she goes roaring on. Her skipper, Lieutenant Commander Montgomery, orders that smoke be laid. At once great clouds of billowing smoke pour out of the PT's stern. Under cover of the smoke, Montgomery turns and fires two torpedoes. In the confusion and smoke, Montgomery and his men cannot be sure what effect the torpedoes have had, but they hear at least one and possibly two explosions which they believe to be hits.

With the second destroyer still after them, they try to shoot out her searchlights and finally manage to discourage the pursuit by dropping depth charges directly in the destroyer's path. At last the 60 boat slips away into the darkness, only to come to grief on an unmarked reef near Sandfly Passage. But the 60 will later be refloated and repaired, so all in all it has been a grand night for the PT's. One cruiser sunk and another cruiser and a destroyer damaged.

•

The fierce naval battles for control of the waters around Guadalcanal were to continue for the next six months and during that time two names become synonymous with PT-boat activities—the Tokyo Express and the Slot.

The Slot was the passage between the islands of New Georgia and Santa Isabel. Japanese reinforcements running south from Rabaul, the great Japanese naval base on New Britain, habitually approached Guadalcanal through the Slot. Night after night they came—cruisers, destroyers, battleships, transports. So regular was their approach that it was almost as if they were running on schedule; therefore, the name Tokyo Express. And night after night the tiny PT's went into action against their vastly stronger foes in the dark waters of the Slot.

The strain on the boats and their crews in those early days of the war was terrific. After fighting all night, the boats returned to base in the early morning and began immediate preparations for going out again as soon as it was dark. This meant field-stripping and lubricating all guns and reloading ammunition belts and clips. It also meant taking aboard some three thousand gallons of gasoline, which usually had to be loaded by hand pumps. This back-breaking job of refueling—in temperatures that hovered around the 100-degree mark—took most of the day, which meant that seldom, if ever, did the crews get more than an hour or two of rest before going out again at night. It was not uncommon in those days to see a PT crewman sound asleep in the fierce glare of the sun on a hard deck, with someone else pounding or scraping something no more than six inches from his ear.

It was now evident that both our people and the enemy had come to realize the climactic importance of the struggle for Guadalcanal. Iron Bottom Bay—between Florida Island and Guadalcanal—became the favorite hunting grounds of the PT's. The method of operation required that PT's be placed as scouts in the entrance channels to the west of Savo Island, where they could report the approach of the Japanese warships. Again we see a resemblance to the old style of Indian fighting, with scouts on speedy ponies hiding behind hillocks or between canyon walls to watch for the approach of the enemy.

On one such night in October 1942, the 39 boat was scouting to the west of Savo Island when its lookouts reported two ships rounding Cape Esperance and heading for Savo at full speed. At that moment a seaplane overhead dropped a flare. In the harsh brilliant light the skipper of 38 boat, patrolling inshore of PT 39, saw the bow of a Japanese destroyer looming over him and just about to cut his boat in two. In the blackness, none of the PT boatmen had seen the approaching destroyer, and if it had not been for the lucky accident of the flare, they would not have had a chance. As it was, the destroyer hesitated long enough to open fire on the plane that had dropped the flare, thus giving the 38 boat the few seconds it needed to accelerate out of the way.

While the 38 boat was twisting and turning in an effort to lose her pursuer—both hurtling at full speed through the blackness—the 39 boat came charging in to the attack and closed to within 400 yards before firing a spread of three torpedoes. In the smoke and confusion, no one can be exactly sure of what happened next, but the men of the 39 boat heard a series of loud explosions which led them to believe that at least one of their fish had scored an amidships hit.

Thus it went, night after night, in cat and mouse maneuvers against the enemy destroyers and cruisers. On the night of November 6, Lieutenant Gamble in PT 48 managed to close to within 400 yards of an enemy destroyer before firing his full load of four torpedoes. Two of them hit the destroyer, sending up a fiery geyser of water and flame.

The following afternoon, every PT that was in condition for action was ordered out to intercept five more Japanese cruisers, which, this time, were reported to be heading straight for Guadalcanal. So low was the squadron on replacement parts at that time that only three boats were available. The 61, the 39, and the 37 went out to meet the line of advancing Japanese destroyers. In the unequal battle which followed, the 39 fired two torpedoes at the lead destroyer, but the 61 was unable to get its fish off because the 37 was in its line of sight. The 37, however, was able to get off three torpedoes of its own. The destroyers meanwhile had opened fire and a shell had struck the 61 boat square on the bow. With nothing much forward of its bridge except a gaping hole, the 61 boat was still able to maintain speed and reach the safety of Tulagi Island. The 39 boat was also damaged by shrapnel but continued the patrol. The entire operation—from first sighting to last—had taken less than eight minutes. It was a typical night operation for the PT's, and when it was over, the squadron was down to its last two boats.

But there was no rest for the weary crews of the PT's and their by now dilapidated boats. The enemy had chosen the second week in November for its mightiest effort to reinforce Guadalcanal—an effort that had to be stopped at all costs.

On November 9, our scout planes reported the Japanese on the move. When our intelligence officers had completed their study of the photos brought back by the scout planes, they were convinced that a gigantic Japanese amphibious operation was under way that might possibly reach Guadalcanal by the night of the thirteenth. Meanwhile, a major force of our own, consisting of more than six thousand men and vast supplies and equipment, was also on its way to the island and had to be unloaded before the thirteenth if the Japanese were not to regain control of Guadalcanal.

The fate of Guadalcanal—and the course of the war— were to be determined by what happened in the twenty-four-hour period before November 13.

On the night of the twelfth, the American and Japanese navies met in one of the bloodiest naval engagements of the war. Five American cruisers and eight destroyers turned to the east to try to stop a superior Japanese force of seventeen ships, which included two battleships and fourteen destroyers. The engagement that followed lasted only thirty-four minutes, but during that time the American Navy suffered staggering losses. In half an hour we lost five ships sunk and three more put out of action. The

Japanese drive was halted, but only for the moment. Their forces were to return again the following night and this time there was only a handful of PT boats to stop them.

The night of November 13 was a night the PT boatmen at Guadalcanal were never to forget.

At midnight the enemy cruisers and destroyers came charging back through Iron Bottom Bay. Two PT's, under the command of Lieutenants Taylor and Searles, were screening the heavy cruiser *Portland,* which had been badly damaged the night before and was dead in the water. It was a typical wet, squally Guadalcanal night. Rain clouds swept down the mountains and across the sea, leaving the PT crews shivering in their thin cotton clothing. Suddenly the sky was lit up by flares, and Lieutenant Taylor reported flashes of gunfire from what was obviously a heavy ship, possibly a battleship. Although the PT was exposed by the flares, Taylor closed in on his target and fired three torpedoes. At least one struck its target. The enemy ship ceased fire at once and began to move slowly away from Guadalcanal. The other PT boat meanwhile had succeeded in putting two torpedoes into one of the Japanese destroyers. The Japanese, not knowing what was attacking them or in what strength, broke off the action. The PT's had clearly had the better of it. For the second night in a row, and this time by only two PT's, the Tokyo Express had been turned back and Guadalcanal and Henderson Field were still ours.

Undoubtedly, this easy victory was achieved because the Japanese did not know how much damage they had inflicted on our fleet the night before and could have had no way of knowing the strength of the force that was now attacking them. If they had known that the entire United

States naval strength being thrown against them at that moment consisted of two wooden PT boats, they would unquestionably have come charging through Iron Bottom Bay. Thus, by surprise and audacity, and without a single casualty, the PT boats achieved a great victory.

Although the Japanese were never again able to mount the major effort that would have been required to drive the American forces from Guadalcanal, the nightly battles in the Slot still went on.

By the first week in December, the strength of the PT's had been bolstered by the arrival of another squadron. On the night of December 7, our patrol planes reported a force of at least nine destroyers moving down the Slot. Eight PT's were ordered out to engage them. In the battle that followed, the nine destroyers were turned back by the eight PT's.

Two nights later, the 59 boat, with Lieutenant Searles at the helm, sighted and sank a 2,000-ton Japanese submarine. And again, on the twelfth, PT's turned back another destroyer force and sank at least one of them, the *Terutsuki*. These sinkings, incidentally, were confirmed by official Japanese documents found after the war.

The PT's at Guadalcanal had surpassed the fondest hopes of their designers and builders. They had succeeded in doing more than anyone had expected of them and had played a key role in what later was regarded as a turning point of the war. But their battles were far from over. On the last night of January, the mosquito boats were involved in what was for them the fiercest engagement of the Guadalcanal campaign.

Earlier in the day, scout planes had reported a force of twenty enemy destroyers heading full speed down the

Slot. Naturally it was assumed that this meant another enemy attempt to reinforce Guadalcanal. As it later developed, this was actually the beginning of the Japanese evacuation, but the American forces had no way of knowing that at the time.

Every available PT was ordered out to meet the new threat. This time the PT's had a real fight on their hands and soon knew it. PT 111 was struck by shellfire from the destroyers and set ablaze. Her skipper, blinded by the flames, was saved by his crewmen, but another officer and enlisted man were lost.

Three other boats, having survived an intensive Japanese air attack, found themselves surrounded and trapped by a dozen destroyers. Caught between the destroyers and the towering coast of Guadalcanal, the PT's had no place to turn. They fought back to the best of their ability, but it would have been all over with them except for a sudden rain squall that allowed them to slip through the ring of steel and so escape the trap.

During that engagement, the 37 boat received a direct hit in her fuel tanks. For the PT-boat skippers, carrying thousands of gallons of high-octane gas in their fragile hulls, this was always a nightmare possibility. Now it became reality for the 37 boat. She exploded in a great white flash that seemed to light up the entire sky. There was only one survivor.

Throughout the night, the fierce battle of the PT's against the destroyer force went on. Only eight of the eleven PT's that had gone out that night came home, and the boats that did come limping home carried heavy casualties. Although the enemy had once more been turned back, there was little joy or elation at the PT base.

There was no more fighting to be done at Guadalcanal. By the end of the first week in February, the Japanese had completed their withdrawal and the tide in the Pacific had turned.

The PT boats and their crews were badly in need of a rest. Few of the boats were now able to maintain the speed which had been their best defense. In many cases they were scarcely faster than, if as fast as, the Japanese destroyers that pursued them. Most of the men had been reduced to wearing the "uniform," or lack of uniform, which was to become more or less standard for PT crews in the Pacific—ragged pants torn off at the knees; the remnants of a shirt, or no shirt; shoes cut out at the toes to give the wearer some relief from the heat.

The men also suffered from tropical fevers—malaria and dengue. To help them resist the fever, they were given Atabrine tablets, which turned their skin as yellow as egg yokes. Although the average age of the PT boatmen could not have been much over eighteen or nineteen, they looked as skinny and yellow as shrunken old men.

The pressure of the Tokyo Express had begun to ease off, but there were still plenty of battles for the PT boats in the Solomons. One such battle has become legendary, for it involved PT 109 and her skipper, Lieutenant (jg) John F. Kennedy.

On the night of August 1, 1943, four enemy destroyers were seen on the west side of Kolombangara Island. Fifteen PT boats went out to meet the destroyers, among them the 109. Suddenly, out of the darkness, there came the glimmer of foam as a destroyer turned and charged straight down on the 109. In a moment she had rammed the boat and the PT burst into flames. Several other PT's attempted to torpedo the destroyer that had sunk the 109, but no hits were scored.

It has been estimated that the destroyer which rammed the future President's boat must have been traveling at a speed of at least forty knots. The PT was split right down the middle. Fortunately for the men who had survived the crash, the gasoline fire was largely on the water instead of on the wreckage, to which the men were clinging.

When Lieutenant Kennedy realized that some of his men had been separated from the others, he left the wrecked hull to which he had been clinging and swam out into the darkness to find the rest of his men.

After three hours of swimming Lieutenant Kennedy and his fellow officers managed to locate and rescue all other survivors. Daylight was beginning to tint the sky, and by this first pale light Kennedy could see that the wrecked hull now lay six or seven miles from land. It was apparent that the wreckage could not remain afloat much longer, and Kennedy realized that this would be his last chance to get his ten men ashore.

You have to visualize the situation in those black waters off that still blacker coast in order to appreciate fully Kennedy's actions. For one thing, imagine the tremendous shock of seeing that steel prow lunge out of the darkness and split his boat in half. Then imagine the terrible uncertainty of not knowing exactly how many of his men had been lost or where they were or whether or not there were sharks in the water.

There was a small island not more than two and a half miles away, but Kennedy thought there might be Japanese on it and decided instead to try for another island a mile or so beyond.

At two o'clock in the afternoon, Kennedy abandoned the sinking PT 109 and struck out with his men for the island. Those who could not swim were towed on a raft by the others. Kennedy himself took a seriously wounded sailor in tow and shepherded him all the way to the beach.

It was almost dark by the time they reached land, but Kennedy did not rest. He went back into the water to try to attract the attention of PT boats heading out on their evening patrols. He set out at about 6:30 and was in the water until almost midnight without seeing any PT's. On the way back, he was swept by the current in a big circle about two miles out into the bay, so that he was at last forced to rest on a reef. When he finally managed to return to his men, he was completely exhausted.

Living only on coconuts, Kennedy and his men somehow managed to survive the next several days. Again and again they made attempts to attract the attention of the PT's, but always without success. At last, on August 8, Lieutenant Kennedy and Ensign Ross made contact with a group of natives, who provided them with food and a canoe. As always in the South Pacific, the natives were extremely kind to Allied soldiers, sailors, and airmen. At last, aided by the natives and an Australian coastwatcher who had been hidden on the island, Kennedy managed to get word to the PT's. Seven days after PT 109 had been rammed by the destroyer, Kennedy and his men, all of whom had long since been given up for dead, returned to their base.

4

The true Black Coast of the war was the huge, ugly, un-explored island of New Guinea. New Guinea is one of the largest islands in the world; it is also the least known. While the rest of the world has been opened up to civilization, New Guinea has remained sunk in brooding silence. There is gold in New Guinea, but no way to get it out. There is oil, but no way to transport it. Its coasts are bound by knife-edged reefs and impenetrable jungle. Its interior is studded with uncrossable mountains that soar 15,000 feet into the air and are lost in freezing mists every day of the year. Its jungles are alive with headhunters. Its dark brown rivers abound in savage crocodiles and poisonous snakes of every description. And over all is the fever—the malarial and dengue fevers that gradually wear down and ultimately kill the white man.

This then was the island that was to be the next great hunting ground of the PT boats and was to occupy more of them longer than any other place.

You may wonder why anybody would fight for New Guinea. Why did the Japanese attack it in the first place? Why did the United States struggle for years, at enormous cost, to regain it?

Because beyond New Guinea lay Australia. Once the Japanese had control of New Guinea, the entire subcontinent of Australia lay before them. Australia was as important to us in the Pacific as England was in Europe. We would fight as hard to defend Australia as we would our own coastline. The great definitive battle for Australia took place in New Guinea.

A map will give you an idea of the enormous size of New Guinea, but nothing short of being there yourself can convey the wildness of its mountains and the horror of its jungle. War is dreadful enough under any circumstances, but on New Guinea it was an everlasting nightmare.

Three months after the attack on Pearl Harbor, while the battle for Corregidor in the Philippines was still raging, the Japanese landed on New Guinea. There were few Allied troops to resist the first advance but the country was so rough that the Japanese were confined largely to the coastal sections and had to supply their men by sea. Two Australian brigades fought one of the most heroic actions of the war and halted the enemy advance, turning it back when the Japanese were less than thirty-five miles from Port Moresby, the last Allied base on New Guinea. Yet even these staunch Australians would have been overcome had the enemy troops been supplied and reinforced. However, the screen of PT boats that prowled the

Black Coast like angry sharks and picked off barges and landing craft managed to blockade the Japanese.

All during those bitter months when the great naval actions of the war were being fought in the south and central Pacific, the PT's were alone in New Guinea. Ragged, often hungry, short of equipment and supplies, the men of the PT's fought an action on the seas that turned the course of the war.

The PT boats were shipped across the Pacific on the decks of tankers, six boats to each tanker. These tankers, loaded with high-octane gas, were floating bombs, and because they did not travel in convoy, they sometimes went so far south to avoid submarines that they found themselves among the ice floes of the Antarctic.

The boats were fastened to the deck in such a way that they could be cast off to float free if the ship sank. The quick-release mechanisms had been carefully devised by the Bureau of Ships, but in practice they did not work well. It was almost impossible to anchor a PT to a ship's deck so that it would remain stationary in a storm at sea and still float free on short notice.

On May 24, 1943, a ship carrying six PT's on its deck was torpedoed about a hundred miles from Noumea. The PT's were cast off but were damaged by contact with the tanker's deck as the water rose. One PT was carried under water by the sinking ship and then bobbed up again like a cork. In the end, two of the PT's were lost, but four, although badly damaged, were able to make it to Noumea and were there repaired and refitted.

When the PT's arrived in Australia, they were off-loaded and, to save wear and tear on their engines, were towed to New Guinea, a distance of more than a thousand miles across the stormy reaches of the Great Barrier Reef. The PT's normally have a quick lively motion, but, weighed down as they were by tow ropes a hundred yards long, the motion was almost unbearable and some of the men who took that long voyage north reached New Guinea twenty-five or thirty pounds lighter and scarcely able to stand.

But reach it they did and some went into action that same night. The opening chapter in the grueling struggle for the southwest Pacific was on.

By the end of February, Squadrons 7 and 8 and the base force personnel of Squadron 6 had arrived in New Guinea and established a base at a pinprick on the map called Kana Kopa. Kana Kopa was a tiny circular bay, no more than 250 yards across, which provided a sheltered harbor for the boats. It was no better or worse than a dozen other such bays which were later used as advance bases. But what has left Kana Kopa etched forever in the memories of the PT men who were there was the mud. Constant, never ending, sticky red mud. Mud so deep, so all-embracing that at one point a good-sized truck with all its load actually sank from view in the mud and disappeared in the middle of the base.

At that time the *Hilo*, a PT tender, had arrived in New Guinea, to make life a little easier for the crews, but drydock and repair facilities were still on the primitive side. Someone had discovered an ancient marine railway on the island of Sariba, and this was now pressed into use for the PT's. The power for the railway was supplied by a group of shaggy-headed Papuans who put their backs to the job of turning an antiquated hand winch. The headman set the pace for the winchwinders by blowing on a conch shell, calling the stroke in the same manner as a coxswain on a racing shell.

The PT crews also improvised in other respects, particularly in regard to food. Ovens were manufactured from used oil drums, and pie plates were made from ammo-box covers. In 1942, in New Guinea, a pie of any kind was a miracle, and if it tasted a little of oil or engine grease, who cared?

The function of the PT boats began to change after they had reached New Guinea. The destroyers that had chased them in the Solomons were no longer in evidence, and the enemy was using barges and landing craft from the great Japanese base at Rabaul. Since this Japanese traffic moved only at night, the PT's were the ideal craft to stop them, and for that purpose they began to change from torpedo boats to gunboats.

The PT's still carried torpedoes but hardly ever fired them. In addition, they now carried a 37 mm. cannon on the foredeck, two sets of twin-mounted .50 caliber machine guns in power-driven turrets, two .30 caliber machine guns on stanchions beside the bridge, a 40 mm. cannon on the stern, and the usual complement of depth charges and torpedoes. Along with these heavy weapons, there was a variety of hand weapons, including submachine guns and rifles. It was necessary, of course, to carry thousands of rounds of ammunition for all these guns, and so, with their load of high-octane gas, the PT's were virtually floating powder kegs that could be ignited by a single spark. It is some sort of minor miracle, and a tribute certainly to the men who manned them, that not more were blown up either accidentally or by enemy fire.

The first boats had arrived in New Guinea in late February and, by early March, were already involved in a decisive battle. On the afternoon of March 1, United States scout planes reported a major enemy convoy in the straits between New Guinea and New Britain. It was made up of eight transports guarded by eight destroyers and was obviously on its way to reinforce New Guinea.

Before this, the Japanese had been operating in the New Guinea area pretty much as they pleased. The only real resistance they had met had been on land, where the Australians had been pushing them back over the incredibly rugged Kokoda Trail. Sometimes the PT crews would see these Aussies, the walking wounded, the ragged, fever-stricken men, hardly more than skin and bones, coming down the trail singing their favorite marching songs, *Waltzing Matilda* and *We're Off to See the Wizard*. The gallantry and courage of the Aussies, fighting under what may have been the most trying conditions of the war, will always be admired by the PT men who saw them in those days.

Now the Japanese in the southwest Pacific were to meet the first serious resistance from sea and air. A hornet's nest of American and Australian planes swarmed out to attack the enemy convoy. Despite the enemy air cover, which was numerically superior, the Allied planes attacked repeatedly all through that long afternoon. The next day bad weather hampered our planes, but during the night the convoy was pursued by flying boats. The day after, the third of March, the battle raged on. By nightfall there were only three enemy destroyers and two transports left afloat. This became known as the Battle of the Bismarck Sea, and its cost to the enemy was staggering. Estimates made after the war indicated that nearly seven thousand

Japanese troops were lost that day. If the enemy had been able to land these men in New Guinea, the entire campaign there would have taken a different course.

By nightfall on the third, the enemy ships were within range of the PT's, and seven PT's set out from the then advance base at Tufi to meet them. Two of the boats were disabled by floating wreckage and had to turn back, but five others closed in for the attack.

Shortly after midnight, the 143 boat fired two torpedoes into a Japanese freighter, the 6,493-ton *Oigawa Maru,* and watched it sink. The other boats patrolled through heavy rain squalls during the night and in the morning saw an unforgettable spectacle. The entire sea, from horizon to horizon, seemed to be covered with a carpet of wreckage and bodies. Hundreds of survivors from the sunken ships were afloat in rafts and rubber boats. The PT skippers were faced then with a terrible decision. They had no room on board their boats to take these enemy soldiers prisoner. Neither could they allow them to get ashore to fight again. The rubber boats and rafts were machine-gunned and depth-charged. It was a harrowing operation which unquestionably left its mark on the men who were there.

At last the grim Battle of the Bismarck Sea was over. The enemy never again attempted to send a major force by daylight to New Guinea. From then on, the great bulk of enemy traffic consisted of barges attempting to slip into the coast under cover of darkness, and there the PT's played a major role in defeating the enemy.

As the function of the PT's became more and more that of gunboats, the enemy also began to change his tactics. To protect his barges, he began to mount shore batteries along the coast. Enemy barges were often used as bait to lure the PT's into traps where they would be exposed to enemy fire. There was hardly a night from that time until the end of the New Guinea campaign that the PT's did not have to run a gauntlet of artillery fire.

One might wonder why the PT's had to come so close to the beach and be exposed to the enemy shore batteries. The answer is that it was the only way they could hunt down the barges. The PT's, patrolling in pairs, would cruise slowly up the coast from their base. If they were outside of the barges, they could not see them against the blackness of the jungle. The only chance of intercepting the barges lay in being inside of them, no matter how close to the beach they came.

This involved a double risk, from the shore batteries and from the razor-sharp coral reefs that stud the Black Coast. Slowly, cautiously, the PT's would creep along, all lookouts straining their eyes for the outline of a barge sometimes barely visible against the sky.

When the barges came, they were usually in groups, and when a cluster of them was sighted, the PT's would turn on full speed and close in with all guns blazing. Many of the barges, sometimes a hundred feet long or more, were armored, and it took a great deal of gunfire to sink them. Torpedoes could not be used against the barges because of their shallow draft; fish fired at them would have passed harmlessly underneath.

As the PT's fired at the barges, the enemy fired back with machine guns mounted on the bows of the barges and with concentrated rifle fire from troops traveling as passengers. In addition to all this, the PT's were exposed to artillery fire from the beach. But round and round they would go at top speed, throwing out phosphorescent bow waves and raking the barges with their tracer fire.

For a few moments the night would be lit up as if by all the fireworks in the world, and then it would be over, with the barges left sinking in the water. As a rule, the PT's were happy enough to escape the fire from the shore, but some skippers had the temerity to close in and shoot it out with the enemy land artillery.

One such skipper was Lieutenant (jg) Joe Burk, a one-time Olympic rowing champion, who, while engaged in attacking barges, was subjected to heavy fire from shore batteries. Burk reversed the usual procedure and calmly closed in on the beach, opening fire on the shore batteries. To the Japanese gunners this must have seemed like a single foot soldier attacking a fortress. Burk cruised back and forth, subjecting the enemy gunners to blistering fire from his automatic weapons, finally silencing the enemy entirely. When he had accomplished this, he returned to the destruction of the barges. For this and other actions Burk received the Navy's top combat award, the Navy Cross.

Burk, at that time a tall, robust, tow-headed youth, is remembered by his classmates at the PT Training Center as a pleasantly unassuming young man. There was no indication that he would turn into a tiger in combat. It is one of the peculiarities of war that there is almost no way to tell by a man's outward appearance or manner how he will behave under fire.

Joe Burk, like all PT officers, was a volunteer. It was not easy to get into the PT's. As a result, the spirit of the men who served in the boats was very high, and their performance against heavy odds and adverse conditions was remarkably good. Burk has been singled out here to illustrate the operation of PT's in silencing enemy shore batteries, but in the nightly patrols of the PT boats there were thousands of other deeds by other men of equally high caliber.

The beginning of the end for the Japanese on the Black Coast of New Guinea had already begun. But they had no way of knowing it. In the months and years that followed, their stubborn efforts to reinforce their units ashore continued. And, as the nature of the war in the southwest Pacific continued to change, so too did the functions of the PT boats. They had been converted to a large extent from torpedo to gun boats, and they were also used on occasion as troop carriers.

On the night of June 29, four PT boats played a major role in the landings at Nassau Bay. Unfortunately, this was one of the most snafued operations of the war in that area. The PT's were to act as a screening force for the landing craft, in addition to which each boat would carry seventy men as a landing force. It was a stormy night, with poor visibility and poorer communications, and the PT's frightened off the landing craft and the landing craft confused the PT's. No one seemed to know exactly what to do. Luckily, the enemy did not oppose the landing. Later attempts at using the PT's as troop carriers were more successful, but even at best, that was hardly the most efficient way to employ these high-speed, fragile craft.

The PT's were also used as liaison with the Australian Coast Watchers. The Coast Watchers were former copra planters who knew the Black Coast and its offshore islands. They had volunteered to go ashore in enemy-held territory to spy on the Japanese and report the movements of their ships and planes.

Imagine the courage it took to be set down alone, or sometimes with just a native boy or two to carry equipment, on a small island full of enemy troops. The PT's were ideal carriers for these Coast Watchers, as they could slip in quickly for a landing under cover of dark and then be gone as quickly. Usually the PT idled as close up to the beach as it dared while the Coast Watcher and his native companion were put ashore in a rubber raft.

That part was not too difficult—the hazardous operation for the Coast Watcher came later. Using shortwave radio equipment, he was expected to report on the movement of Japanese shipping along the coasts. As soon as the Coast Watcher began using his radio, the Japanese would home in on his signal and begin to hunt him down. Often they used dogs for this purpose, sweeping through the jungle examining every tree and bush and cave. The Coast Watcher, like a cornered animal, ran back and forth in ever narrowing circles and still managed to keep up a flow of invaluable information.

When the PT's put the Coast Watchers ashore, they made arrangements to come back for them on a certain night two or three weeks later. Sometimes the Coast Watchers were at the rendezvous point; more often they were not. The activities of these heroic men were kept secret during the war, and it was only afterward that something came to be known of their operations and of the part the PT's played in assisting them.

The standard "bread and butter" operations of the PT's, however, were their nightly battles with the enemy barges.

On the night of July 28, two PT's found themselves suddenly in the midst of thirty or more heavily laden enemy barges heading across the straits between New Britain and New Guinea. As was often the case along the Black Coast, a succession of heavy squalls blew down from the steep mountains and visibility was limited to a few yards.

Suddenly the PT commanders saw dark forms all around them and realized that they were right in the middle of an enemy formation. Some of the Japanese barges were no more than ten or fifteen feet away and attempted to ram the PT's. The PT's at once opened fire. The blackness was pierced by tracers and above the sound of the rain came the flat, hammering chatter of guns. It was almost impossible to tell friend from foe, but the PT's had an advantage in being so badly outnumbered—almost anything they shot at was bound to be the enemy. An enemy 20 mm. shell exploded in the engine room of one of the PT's, putting two of its engines out of action, but when the engagement was finally broken off, a good many of the barges were left sinking.

Another job which was turned over to the PT's at this time was the strafing of enemy-held villages along the coast. Guns of every description were brought into play for this operation. On some occasions even trench mortars were mounted on the bows of the PT's. The use of mortars sometimes produced interesting results. Mortars—unlike cannon, which have a flat trajectory—travel in an extremely high curve, and occasionally the enemy antiaircraft guns would open a wild barrage against the sky, thinking that the shells dropping on them were bombs from allied planes. On the night of August 23, PT's strafing the shore saw, by the light of their exploding shells, two barges on the beach. The barges were set afire and burned with such fury that when the PT's were thirty miles away they could still see the red glow against the sky.

Another unorthodox use of PT's involved the collecting of intelligence, that is, information pertaining to the enemy's movements. This was usually relayed by the Papuans, who would paddle out in their canoes to meet the PT's. Almost without exception, the natives of New Guinea —who had so recently been, and in some cases still were, headhunters—were friendly to the Allied forces and did their best to aid them. The Japanese forces had made the initial error of treating the natives with arrogance and cruelty. It was a costly mistake.

It is interesting to speculate on what these savages— most of whom had never before seen a plane or car— must have thought when the great waves of wartime mechanized equipment began pouring ashore. If it impressed them, they gave no sign of it, remaining always stiff-faced and inscrutable. But they quickly adapted to the new ways, and soon there was hardly a village, no matter how remote, that was not using empty gas cans for cooking purposes. When the war ended, great masses of spare parts, up to and including aircraft engines, were abandoned in the jungle, on the theory that it would be too expensive to transport them back. Even today the Papuans are undoubtedly still using whatever is left of this wartime debris.

Often, too, the PT crews, armed with submachine guns and rifles, would go ashore in swift commando-like raids that sometimes netted valuable information from Japanese-held villages. It was from letters and documents captured in such raids that the PT commanders really began to understand the extent to which their destruction of enemy barges was turning the tide of war in the southwest Pacific.

5

Now that the Japanese drive toward Port Moresby had been halted, it was time for the Allied ground forces in New Guinea to go on the offensive. By the first week in September, Australian forces were pouring ashore on the beaches east of Lae. Within three days, nearly 15,000 men had been landed there and had begun their drive west to take the major enemy bases of Lae and Salamaua. At the same time paratroopers were dropping out of the skies behind Nadzeb and moving down the Markham Valley from the west.

These interior sections of New Guinea are primitive and largely unexplored. Pilots who have flown over the jungles have even claimed to have sighted strange prehistoric monsters in the deep valleys between the mountains. Whether or not dinosaurs still roam the wilds of New

Guinea remains undetermined, but imagine, if you can, the eerie, centuries-old stillness into which the paratroopers dropped, and imagine the utter blackness of this coast along which the PT's patrolled.

As many boats were lost on uncharted reefs in those early months of the New Guinea campaign as ever were lost in enemy action. So frequently did this occur that a standard procedure was followed. While the crew of the boat that had gone aground was swimming to another PT, which was standing by, the skipper would remain behind to blow up his boat. This was usually done by opening the gas tanks and tossing a hand grenade down the companionway. That this method was not without danger was demonstrated on the night of June 24, when PT 193 went hard aground on a reef off Noemfoor Island. When all attempts to refloat her failed, her skipper, Lieutenant C. R. Taylor, a brave officer who had survived many of the fierce actions of the New Guinea campaign, got his men off and stayed behind to blow up his ship. Unhappily he was caught below decks by a premature explosion and was fatally burned.

With the Japanese now on the defensive, the PT base was moved northwest along the coast to Morobe. Here the boats were moored along the banks of the Morobe River, with camouflage nets strung overhead to hide them from the Japanese scout planes that were continually searching out PT nesting areas. The dreadful heat of the secluded backwaters and muddy rivers was almost indescribable, and as in the Solomons, most of the men were suffering from tropical fevers and gaping ulcers.

Although Atabrine was reasonably helpful in combating malaria, nothing seemed to be proof against the ulcers. Any slight bruise on the arm or leg—and the men in PT's were continually being bruised by the rough action of the boats —would eventually result in an ulcer or sore that lasted weeks and often months. Potassium permanganate, a purple dye, was used to treat the ulcers. It was not unusual to see the members of a PT-boat crew sporting purple splotches from head to foot like so many painted savages.

As the focus of the war moved farther west, the boats were compelled to extend the range of their patrols. Boats leaving Morobe often had to travel a hundred miles or more along the coast before reaching their patrol stations. Since the boats could move only at night, so as to avoid Japanese bombers, this meant a four- or five-hour high-speed trip through rough seas to reach the beginning of the patrol area. The wear and tear on the boats and their crews can readily be imagined. It was not unheard of for an unwary passenger on the PT's to return with both legs broken, because he had failed to brace himself properly during one of the wild rides along the coast.

Despite the difficulties, the PT's were now inflicting heavy damage on the enemy. In November alone, the PT's sank forty-five enemy barges. When you consider that the barge traffic was now the enemy's last remaining means of supplying his forces on New Guinea, you can appreciate what the loss of forty-five barges in a single month must have meant.

It was at this time—in the fall of 1943—that PT's had their only encounter with enemy destroyers along the New Guinea coast. And a rough one it was.

On the night of October 8, two boats—the 128 and the 194—were patrolling off the coast of New Britain, across the Vitiaz Strait from New Guinea, when they were surprised by a flotilla of enemy destroyers. The first shell fired by the enemy from a range of three and a half miles landed less than a boat's length from the 194, throwing every man on board to the deck. This first explosion was followed by three more, all equally close and all so fast that the PT's were unable to get off a shot.

The PT's managed to scoot away at a speed of forty knots, only to find the destroyers close behind. The 194 was held in the blue-white glare of a searchlight beam, which her gunners finally managed to shoot out by pumping round after round of 40 mm. shells at the enemy.

In order to split the enemy's fire, the PT's swung in opposite directions—the 128 heading north and the 194 south. But twist and turn as the 194 might, she could not escape the enemy's remarkably accurate fire. Another five-inch shell had landed within fifteen feet of her transom, piercing the hull with shrapnel and killing two men.

Both PT's had been laying smoke from their smoke generators, but when the skipper of the 194 ordered the smoke secured, it was found that the smoke generator valve had stuck. Instead of hiding the PT, it was giving the enemy a point on which to concentrate his fire. One of the officers seized a fire ax and chopped the smoke bottle loose, kicking it over the side. At the same time, the two PT's again changed course.

This was very nearly their last maneuver, for as the two boats came roaring through the clouds of smoke, they found themselves plunging head on into each other. At the last moment the wheels were put hard over, and though the PT's did actually collide, leaving each with a shattered bow, the blows were glancing and the boats were able to continue on at full speed until at last they lost the pursuing destroyers behind the lee of Sakar Island.

•

The Japanese in New Guinea were starving. Evidence of this came from captured Japanese diaries which described the shortage of food. It could also be seen in the Japanese dead. The Japanese had apparently been subsisting largely on a diet of native roots and berries. Famished Japanese prisoners of war were being taken in increasing numbers and they told their captors that a three days' supply of rice was now expected to last the better part of two weeks. In addition it was learned that the enemy had slaughtered almost all of their pack animals for food. This seriously handicapped them in the transport of guns and munitions. The iron blockade thrown along the Black Coast by the PT's was beginning to pay off.

The Japanese were now making frenzied efforts to supply their troops. As well as the barges, they employed a variety of odd submarine-like craft, one of which was sunk just before Christmas by two PT's on patrol off Gneisenau Point. Although the PT's could not see the craft very clearly, in the darkness it appeared to be about a hundred feet long and was unloading stores on the beach. The PT's opened fire and heard a loud hissing noise as though a great quantity of compressed air was escaping from the submersible. It settled in shallow water and the PT's returned to base. A few weeks later, when American ground forces reached Gneisenau Point, they discovered the wrecked craft lying on the bottom. It was not a true submarine at all, but a sort of underwater barge designed to be towed behind a mother sub. This was somewhat like towing gliders behind aircraft, and while it was an ingenious idea, it was not, at least in this case, successful.

The following day, however, the PT's ran into something far more serious. For some weeks the boats had been patrolling across the Vitiaz Strait between New Guinea and New Britain in an attempt to intercept barges in open water. As an incidental duty, they often transported wounded soldiers from the beachhead at Arawe to the Army hospital in New Guinea. On Christmas day, while carrying a group of seriously wounded men, two PT's were caught in daylight by a flight of twenty enemy dive bombers attacking directly out of the sun.

It was the first time in many months that PT's had been caught in so awkward a position by enemy aircraft. As the planes came roaring in on them, and as the bombs began to throw up great white geysers of spray, the PT gunners opened fire against what seemed to be a skyful of whirling, darting planes. Time after time the planes peeled off for an attack and time after time the boats were miraculously saved by near misses. Both boats were holed by flying shrapnel, but neither was so seriously damaged that it was unable to operate. At last, after one of the bombers had gone smoking into the water, the planes drew away.

Next day, however, the battle between the PT's and the planes was resumed. This time the attack was even more violent. Forty or more Japanese dive bombers and fighters bombed and strafed PT's 190 and 191. This engagement was probably the most fierce battle fought between PT's and planes. The two PT's should have been wiped out almost at once by the overwhelming superiority of the enemy force, but as it turned out, the PT's made a mighty elusive target.

Turning and twisting like water bugs in the rough seas, the PT's, with throttles open as far as they would go, dashed backward and forward, hurling shells into the sky, as wave after wave of enemy planes came roaring in. Considering the conditions under which their guns were being aimed, the PT gunners performed miracles of marksmanship that day, shooting down four enemy planes and damaging several others.

The PT's did not go unmarked. The skipper of PT 191 was badly wounded and was replaced at the wheel by his second in command, who was in turn wounded but managed to maneuver the boat to avoid a direct hit. The boat was peppered with chunks of flying metal, which eventually pierced the water jackets of the engines. With hot water and steam spurting out of the engines, the boat would soon have been dead in the water, had it not been for the swift action of one of the mechanics. Despite the rain of bomb splinters and bullets, he stuck to his post and managed to tape up the jackets sufficiently to keep the boat moving.

Shortly thereafter, a flight of American fighters appeared and drove off the remaining enemy planes, but the victory clearly belonged to the PT's. They had demonstrated once again that well-handled boats with sufficient fire power could cope with almost any combination of aircraft thrown against them. Never again did PT's and enemy planes tangle in so wide open a dogfight.

The PT's were not so lucky in what for them was one of the great tragedies of the war—a case of mistaken identity, when they were bombed and strafed by Allied planes.

On the morning of March 27, three PT's were outside the reefs at Bangula Bay when they saw a group of RAAF fighters approaching. The boats were in radio contact with the planes and had clearly established their identity with visual and radio recognition signals, when they were suddenly and mistakenly attacked by another group of Australian planes.

The PT's, recognizing that the planes were friendly, held their fire, but even so, the P-40's kept boring in. One P-40, realizing the tragic error of his comrades, made frantic efforts to call off the attack, but it was too late. The defenseless PT's were burned and sunk, with the loss of four officers and four enlisted men. Four other officers and eight enlisted men were seriously wounded. This loss was greater than any suffered in combat against enemy aircraft.

Terrible as this mistake was, it was to happen again, and all too soon. Four weeks later, the PT's were again attacked in daylight by friendly aircraft. In this case the attack came from carrier-based Marine Corps Corsairs, which swooped down on PT 350 while it was engaged in trying to free PT 347 from a reef.

The Corsair attack began at seven o'clock in the morning, and this time the PT's fought back. In the ensuing battle, one of the planes was shot down and three men were killed on board PT 350. The pilot of the remaining plane had meanwhile radioed for help, claiming that he was engaged in a struggle with two enemy gunboats. All the PT's carried great white stars on their foredecks, and it is very hard to believe that at some point the pilot of the remaining Corsair was not aware of these identification marks. But apparently he was not. In short order, twenty-six more Marine planes arrived and continued to bomb and strafe the PT's.

Meanwhile, PT 346 had arrived to rescue the survivors of the first attack. The commander of 346 saw the additional Corsairs arriving and took it for granted that they had come to serve as air cover. The planes, however, immediately resumed the attack against the PT's, this time in great strength. One more plane was shot down and the last two PT's were destroyed. Fortunately, a Catalina scout plane was able to rescue thirteen survivors of the PT's, but by the time that black day was over, three more PT officers, 11 PT enlisted men, and two of the Corsair pilots were dead.

A Navy court-martial board later concluded that the fault lay with the pilots, who not only had failed to recognize the boats but were operating inside an area that had been barred to them by Intelligence orders.

•

Once the Japanese had been turned back from their drive on Port Moresby, the new policy of the Allies became apparent: to leapfrog up the coast, thus isolating major units of the enemy. It was spring now—the burning, humid spring of New Guinea that is really no different from the rest of the year—and there was a sense of urgency. The war was speeding up. By mid-April, landings had been made at Aitape nearly five hundred miles to the northwest of the old PT base at Dregar. Fifty thousand troops of the 18th Imperial Japanese Army had been cut off by this great leapfrogging jump and could be supplied only by barges. The last great effort of the New Guinea campaign was about to be made, and the PT's were to see more action in the next few months than at any other time.

Never before had the Japanese made so determined an effort to defend their barge traffic. Shore batteries were everywhere, and there was scarcely a night when the PT's were not exposed to increasingly heavy fire from the beach. Although much of this cannonading was from fixed artillery, a greater proportion came from mobile field guns which could be quickly moved from place to place, so that the PT's were never able to determine just when and where they might encounter fire from the shore batteries.

The PT's were in violent action every night. Within a period of three months the boats operating out of Aitape sank almost a hundred enemy barges. It was as if a giant hand were squeezing an artery and slowly cutting off the blood supply to the enemy's heart. Thousands of Japanese troops were destroyed along with the barges and almost all of their supplies of food and ammunition. The Imperial Army's drive to retake Aitape had been blunted and turned back. More and more starving prisoners were being taken.

Prisoners were seldom taken on board a PT. For one thing, there was no room, and, for another, most Japanese fought to the end. Often, when a barge had been sunk, enemy soldiers would be seen floating in the water. The PT crews would fish for the Japanese soldiers with long boathooks, but usually without success. The Japanese preferred to drown or to blow themselves up with hand grenades. The only way a Japanese swimming away from his sinking barge could be taken prisoner was by being clubbed over the head and dragged aboard.

One of the most remarkable actions of those last days of the New Guinea campaign came in late September of 1944. The PT base received word that a Navy pilot in Wasile Bay had been shot down and was still afloat, but that the fire from nearby shore batteries was so intense that rescue was impossible. Despite the fact that other planes had already attempted to land near him and had been driven off, Lieutenant Preston, commander of PT Squadron 33, volunteered to make another try.

This rescue attempt in Wasile Bay was from every standpoint an extraordinary performance. To begin with, knowing how hazardous the action would be, Preston asked that only volunteers accompany him. No man on either of the two boats, the PT 489 and the PT 363, hesitated. Once the boats and their crews had been selected, Preston gave them a hurried briefing. They would have to pass through the entrance that was guarded by big guns. In addition, they would have to traverse minefields. And all this without benefit of surprise. The downed pilot, Ensign Thompson, had been in the water for some time. A rubber raft had been dropped to him and was now aground only two hundred yards from the enemy-occupied beach. Obviously the Japanese gunners could have picked Thompson off whenever they felt like it, but they were using him for bait. And the PT's were coming straight into the trap.

When the PT's were still four miles from the entrance to the bay, a heavy gun opened fire on them from the western shore. At once Preston changed course eastward, traversing as he did so the enemy minefields, but this brought the boats under fire from three more heavy guns on the eastern shore. The two boats, circling at high speed between the shell bursts, were forced back. Out of range of the big guns, they regrouped and made another attempt to force the entrance.

This time they came straight in at maximum speed, disregarding the increasingly heavy fire from the enemy guns. It may have been the very daring of the attempt that saved them. The enemy gunners probably could not believe that two PT's would be used in a suicidal effort to save the life of a single pilot. Or possibly it was the speed of the PT's that was deceptive. At any rate, in they came like arrows hurled from a bow, straight through the entrance, with the Japanese guns now firing at them from every direction.

The scene inside the bay was like something out of a nightmare: Japanese guns firing and the surface of the water pockmarked with continuous shell bursts—aircraft overhead—and the PT's firing back for all they were worth. The downed pilot, on his little rubber raft, was in the middle of it all.

PT 489 now closed in on the raft only a few hundred yards from the beach. The PT was so close to the shore that it was difficult for the enemy to depress his big guns low enough. And of course the PT was hurling back a withering fire of its own which undoubtedly affected the accuracy of the enemy gunners.

Because the raft with the pilot was in shallow water, it was necessary for the PT to stand by while one of its men dived over the side to tow the raft back to the boat. Actually it was two men—Lieutenant Seaman and Motor Machinist O'Day—who performed this heroic service. They were in the water little more than five minutes, but it must have seemed like hours to them and to the men on the

PT's, who were fully exposed to the enemy fire during that time.

Eventually the men towing the raft got back to 489, and the pilot was taken aboard. At once the PT's turned and headed back for the entrance. If anything, the enemy fire was even more intense now. Back and forth the two boats darted and at last made a dead run straight for the Narrows and slipped through. They had been under continuous shellfire in broad daylight for two and a half hours and had suffered only light damage from shrapnel. Home they went.

This action, one of the most skillful and daring rescues of the war, earned for Preston the Medal of Honor, which was awarded to him by President Harry S. Truman.

There would be more fighting in the New Guinea campaign, more barges to be sunk, more PT's damaged and lost, but the enemy had expended the last of its once great strength and the focus of the war was shifting elsewhere.

The Black Coast would never again be quite so black, and the PT's, which had played so vital a part in strangling the Imperial Army's lifelines, were ready to move on.

6

▼

During the final months of the New Guinea campaign, another group of PT's was heavily engaged with an enemy many thousands of miles away. In April 1943 the first American PT's were unloaded at the great British base of Gibraltar and traveled from there under their own power across the tip of the Mediterranean to the north coast of Africa. There they were rushed into service against the German and Italian naval forces operating along the coast.

This turned out to be a different sort of war for the PT's from the one that was being fought in the Pacific. The Pacific war was a grinding, desperate, nightly struggle to wear down a stubborn enemy and starve him into submission. The PT actions in European waters, on the other hand, were more widely spaced and fought not so much with guns as with torpedoes against the German and Italian coastal shipping.

By the middle of 1943 the North African campaign—during which control of the coast had changed hands many times—was drawing to a close, and the PT's were put into service to do as much damage as possible to the Germans if they attempted to evacuate their ground forces by sea. In these battles, the PT's were to encounter for the first time the feared German E boats—a somewhat larger version of the PT, twenty-six feet longer and carrying about the same type of armament. Also, as the Mediterranean campaign continued, they were to encounter the high-speed Italian MAS boats and other, oddly assorted craft such as human torpedoes.

The first action for the PT's came on the night of May 8 in Ras Idda Bay on the coast of Algeria. It was a black, starless night when three British MTB's and the American PT 206 slipped inside the entrance to the bay. Visibility was a quarter of a mile or less, but the Americans had the good fortune to find themselves almost at once facing a prime target: a good-sized German tanker.

The outline of the ship was barely visible against the rocky promontory. With muffled engines, the PT slowly circled its target to find a better angle at which to shoot. There was a breathless hush during which the crew expected at any moment that the sky would be illuminated by searchlights and shore batteries, but Ras Idda Bay remained enveloped in black silence.

The PT slid forward, the only sound being the throaty bubbling at her stern. Now, at last, she was in position. Her skipper pressed the firing switch of his port forward torpedo, and the great gleaming fish twelve feet long slid out of its tube and plopped into the water. As every man on board watched intently, the phosphorescent line of the torpedo's wake lengthened into an arrow aimed straight at the tanker. A few seconds later there was a savage explosion and bits of wreckage were hurled up into the sky and rained down on the PT's decks. The first torpedo fired by a PT in the European theater had run hot, straight, and true.

The PT now turned to search for other targets, but instead her lookouts were horrified to see the wake of two torpedoes heading straight for her. The only thing that saved the 206 that night was her shallow draft; both torpedoes passed directly underneath her, without touching. It later turned out that they had been fired by one of the British MTB's, which in the darkness had mistaken the PT for an enemy ship. Recognition in utter darkness was to be a major problem.

It became an even bigger problem two nights later when PT's were fired upon by British destroyers in the Gulf of Tunis. The PT's had been warned that friendly destroyers were operating in the area and had gone well out of their way to avoid them, but even so, they suddenly found themselves under intensive machine-gun fire from the British. Speeding up and laying smoke, the PT's attempted to escape and in so doing ran into a nest of German E boats. If the situation had been confusing before, it was chaos now, with the PT's, the destroyers, and the E boats firing in all directions, and none of them quite sure which was the enemy.

The 204 boat, under the command of Lieutenant (jg) Clifford, had turned back through the smoke to engage one of the E boats. In so doing, Clifford ran the risk of being sunk by the friendly destroyers, but this was the PT's first fight with an E boat and he was out to make the most of it. Twisting and turning through the smoke, he dashed up alongside the E boat and strafed it with every gun on board. At once the destroyers, which were firing on friend and foe alike, pursued him, but he managed to slip away again into the smoke, leaving the E boat burning. For nearly an hour after that, the PT's were pursued by the destroyers before finally losing them in the darkness. All in all, that night's work must be reckoned as a considerable victory for the PT's.

However, it would be unfair to give the impression that PT's were under constant harassment from Allied guns. Anyone who has operated a boat at night in strange waters even in peacetime will be well aware of what tricks the eyes and the imagination can play. Rocks can look like submarines, and submarines can look like four-masted schooners, and buoys can look like barber poles. The night is a strange and eerie time to be at sea, but night was the time when the PT's did all their roaming, and they soon learned never to take friend or foe for granted. For the most part, though, the British MTB's worked very closely with the American PT's in the European theater, and they were of great help to each other. The British MTB skippers had been at war against the Germans for four years, and their experience was invaluable to the newly arrived Americans.

Not all missions were against the E boats. As in the Pacific, the PT's here were pressed into service on secret voyages involving the landing of spies and saboteurs deep in enemy-held territory. Usually these missions were undertaken for the OSS, and some meant enormous runs of

500 miles or more from the PT base at Bizerte in North Africa across the Mediterranean to the Italian island of Sardinia. The boats had to adopt the dangerous practice of carrying extra drums of fuel on deck. Gasoline is highly explosive, and to carry many hundreds of gallons in drums on deck was a little like carrying dynamite. But the PT's accepted the risk and got away with it. None was blown up by its own fuel.

Gasoline was not the only problem on these long-range missions. There was always the danger of being caught out by German or Italian planes, as on the night of June 11, off the coast of Sicily.

The warm, swift Mediterranean dusk had just settled down, and three PT's, along with a division of British MTB's, were patrolling between Pantelleria and Sicily. The attack came without warning, and the advantage, because of the poor light, was with the planes. In a moment the water was torn by bomb bursts and the boats were enveloped in clouds of smoke and spray. The boats took what evasive action they could, but in the gloom it was impossible for them to make out their attackers until they were directly overhead, by which time of course the bombs were already on the way down.

There were at least eight planes in the attacking force—dive bombers mostly—using delayed-action bombs that exploded underwater like mines. The great hammer blows of the underwater explosions rocked the boats, bending propellers and rudders and sometimes spraying shrapnel across the decks. The thunder of the PT's guns rang out across the darkening sea, and at last the dive bombers gave it up and pulled away. A seaman on one of the boats was dead from a throat wound, but otherwise the boats suffered little damage and were able to continue with the patrol. In the morning they closed in on an Italian boat trying to escape from Pantelleria and took several prisoners.

•

By the middle of July, PT's were involved in the first great Allied naval action of the Mediterranean—the invasion of Sicily. A huge task force had been assembled for the occasion, made up of more than 3,200 ships, boats, and various landing craft. It was the first time in the war that PT's had been made part of so large a force. They were given the job of driving off the E boats that might attack the flanks of the landing force.

As it turned out, the most formidable enemy the PT's had to contend with on the night of July 10 was the weather. The western Mediterranean is famous for sudden squalls, and by midnight the PT's were wallowing through heavy seas fifteen feet high. PT's, being high-speed planing hulls, do not behave well under such conditions, and for the eight boats involved, it was a long grim night of beating up against heavy seas without so much as a sight of the E boats. Possibly the weather was too bad for the Germans, or they may have been withdrawn as part of the general evacuation of Sicily. Whatever the reason, they were nowhere in evidence, and the PT's had the stormy, wind-torn Mediterranean to themselves.

A few nights later, however, the PT's were to encounter stiff resistance when they tangled with three Italian MAS boats. These were a larger, faster, and more heavily gunned version of the MAS boats that had been used in

World War I. They were sixty feet long and carried two torpedo tubes and a cluster of machine guns. They were a few knots faster than the PT's and, perhaps because of their narrower shape, somewhat more maneuverable. As a rule, in boat to boat engagements, the PT's had the advantage of their great weight of guns. However, in this particular battle, when the PT's attacked a group of lighters protected by MAS boats, PT 218 was badly damaged and three of her officers were wounded. The boat's skipper, Lieutenant Arbuckle, although himself wounded, performed heroically, saving his sinking boat and bringing it back to the destroyer base at Palermo. For his actions that night he received the Silver Star.

By now the campaign in the Mediterranean was accelerating. Soon the PT's would be engaged in one of the great naval actions of the war—the invasion of Italy. The Allied forces made their landings at Salerno and Anzio without meeting much initial resistance, but as they attempted to break out of their beachheads, the German pressure stiffened. Slowly and painfully our land forces advanced toward Rome and the strongly fortified Gustav Line, which the enemy had established behind the Rapido River.

For a while it seemed that the Germans might decide to withdraw from Italy altogether, but they soon made it clear that they were out to fight for every last inch of it. It was that fight which gave the PT's along the coast a role of prime importance.

In some ways the position of the Germans in Italy was comparable to that of the Japanese in New Guinea. Italy has an enormously long coastline, and the Germans were using a great deal of waterborne traffic to supply their forces. The PT's were pressed into service to try to halt that traffic as they had done in New Guinea.

The principal enemy of the PT's in Italy was the F-lighter (Flak lighter). These were more than twice the size of the PT's and far more heavily armed. In addition, they were so well built and compartmented that it was impossible to sink them by gunfire. It required a direct hit by a torpedo to send an F-lighter to the bottom, but the F-lighters operated in shallow water under the protection of shore guns and so were seldom in an exposed position for a torpedo run. The F-lighter was a formidable foe, the toughest the PT's had yet encountered.

In addition to the difficulty of fighting the F-lighters, the PT's were now meeting extremely heavy weather. Operating along the Italian coast south of Genoa, they were exposed to the great winter storms for which the Gulf of Genoa is notorious. It was not unusual for them to be struggling through forty-knot winds and twenty-foot seas.

Despite these difficulties and dangers, the boats acquitted themselves well that winter. Working along with the British MTB's, they racked up a score of fifteen F-lighters sunk and many more damaged. The Germans, like the Japanese in New Guinea, were being denied the use of the coastline. They were forced to send their men and supplies overland, where they were exposed to constant attack from low-flying Allied planes.

By late May, better weather had come to the Mediterranean and PT activity began to pick up. The Germans were throwing a new and deadlier foe into the coastal war —the corvette—a sort of pocket-sized destroyer. These ships were fast, heavily armed, and exceedingly dangerous for the flimsy PT's, yet the PT's did not hesitate to sweep in and sting the enemy whenever possible.

On the night of May 23, a PT scouting force tangled with two German corvettes southbound along the coast of Italy. The PTs' fighting abilities had been vastly improved by the addition of radar and a new type of torpedo. The conditions—a calm sea and an exceptionally black night—favored the PT's as they closed in on their targets. Round and round went the radar sweep hand until the radarman on the lead boat spotted the two little silver bugs that meant a target. He watched them for a moment to confirm his finding and then in a whisper passed the word to the bridge.

The skipper of the 202 boat left his wheel for a moment and looked down into the pilothouse to check the radarman's observation. He watched as the sweep hand moved slowly around the circular screen and then saw it blur for a moment on the two blips. Picking up his microphone, he called out, "Red Leader to Warriors. Red Leader to Warriors. I have two targets at range twelve miles bearing 070. We will close immediately."

In a moment the affirmative response from the boats behind him came through and the PT's began to sweep in for the attack. On they went through the blackness until lookouts reported the first visual contact. Now they had to work in a matter of seconds, for if they could see the Germans there was no doubt the Germans would soon be able to see them. With a series of splashes like big fish jumping, torpedoes were rolled out of racks and dropped into the water. Off they went, hissing and burbling. Two minutes later there was a great burst of yellow light in the darkness, and the flat, drumlike impact of an explosion sweeping across the sea.

Although the lead corvette had undoubtedly been struck by one or more torpedoes, the second opened fire, forcing the PT's to retreat out of range. One of the corvettes was definitely out of action, but the other was still blasting shells into the night at a tremendous rate as the PT's closed in again to attack. This time, against a thoroughly alerted opponent, they were able to approach no closer than a mile from the target, but even so, they managed to score a hit.

The water was now full of Germans crying for help. The PT's rescued nineteen of the enemy, who were swimming blindly in the darkness, and learned from them that the leading corvette had gone down after two torpedo hits and that the second enemy ship had been badly damaged and had lost nine men blown over the side. Enemy records show that the second corvette, although it remained afloat and managed to reach the coast at Leghorn, was so badly damaged that it later had to be stripped and abandoned. The PT's, although certainly outweighed, had scored a victory.

How painful losses of this type were to the Germans can be judged from a message intercepted on May 24, from the German Naval Command in Italy, saying that unless something could be done to stop the PT's, the whole system of coastal supply would have to be abandoned.

A week later the PT's, this time in full moonlight, were again in action. The targets were a destroyer and a corvette. Unhappily the moonlight was no friend to the PT's that night. Revealed by the bright light, they were unable to approach by surprise. In a few moments a furious fight had developed.

With all guns blazing, the PT's swept past their larger opponents but did not escape without damage. The 307 boat was badly hit. It managed to keep afloat and retire into the darkness, but it had lost three men killed and five wounded. Even then, it continued to pump 40 mm. shells toward the enemy. It was later learned from prisoners of war that the enemy destroyer had lost two men killed and at least a dozen wounded.

The exchange that night could hardly be considered a victory but the PT's were able to improve their score two weeks later when there was no moon. On a clear warm night off the coast at La Spezia, the PT's carried out a textbook attack against two enemy corvettes. Picking up their targets on radar, the PT's crept undetected to firing position and released their torpedoes. For once the fish ran hot, straight, and true. The leading corvette vanished in a tremendous explosion that was followed moments later by an explosion on the second ship. The second corvette did manage to get off some gunfire, but it was not anywhere near the PT's, which would seem to indicate that it never even saw its attackers. Everything had worked perfectly for the PT's and it was perhaps their best attack of the Mediterranean war. Enemy records later showed both corvettes had been sunk.

7

Shortly after the Allied invasion of southern France, the PT's moved their base of operations to ports along the French Riviera. This is surely one of the pleasantest places in the world in peacetime, and even in wartime it offered none of the hardships known to the PT-boat crews in the southwest Pacific. But if malaria and dengue fever were unheard of at Saint-Tropez, there were plenty of other things to worry the unwary PT skipper—among them the enemy's explosive boats and human torpedoes.

The explosive boats were built of plywood and measured about eighteen feet long and carried as much as 700 pounds of explosives. Sometimes they were manned by an operator, who jumped overboard after aiming the boat at a target. More often they were unmanned and guided by radio from a control vessel. Imagine what an eerie sight they must have made, these crewless, water-borne bombs speeding out of the night at twenty-five knots or more.

The first major contact came on the night of August 26. Two PT's were on patrol duty a few miles from the beach when lookouts suddenly saw a string of five small boats, very low in the water, heading straight for them. The alarm was given and the PT's maneuvered out of the way. The enemy boats continued on in weird silence and without a change of course while the PT's dropped delayed-action flares ahead of them. As the flares ignited, the enemy craft were sharply illuminated and the PT's opened fire. Four of the strange craft blew up in a series of explosions, but it was impossible to tell if they had been exploded by gunfire from the PT's or by radio signals from the control vessel.

A few nights later, PT's again encountered explosive boats, this time three of them speeding toward the beach at thirty knots. The PT's gave chase and gradually closed the range. Suddenly one of the boats stopped dead in the water and blew up while the others changed course and headed straight for the PT's. The PT's separated and let the strange silent craft pass between them, after which it also blew up.

More fantastic even than the explosive boats were the human torpedoes. These were, in effect, two torpedoes in one, the upper having no warhead but containing a plastic dome in which sat the operator who was to guide the lower torpedo to its target and then release it. These strange craft moved slowly through the water at a speed of no more than four knots but in deadly silence.

On the morning of September 9, after a night of battling explosive boats, the PT's suddenly found themselves surrounded by human torpedoes heading toward two American destroyers maneuvering close to the beach. The PT's closed the range and easily destroyed the torpedoes by gunfire. Most of the operators jumped overboard and were picked up by the PT's, but some went down with their craft. In no case were the explosive boats or human torpedoes able to inflict damage on the PT's.

Another strange assignment for the PT's at that time concerned the disposal of the old-style Mark 8 torpedoes. These torpedoes were now considered obsolete, and it was determined that the best way to get rid of them would be to fire them into enemy-held harbors. The harbors of Vado and Port Maurizio were chosen for the experiment. At midnight, idling well offshore, the PT's let go their fish in the general direction of the crowded harbors. A series of very loud explosions were heard, which, it was later learned, coincided with a partisan uprising ashore. The bewildered Germans, unable to tell where the attack was coming from, fired blindly in all directions without hitting anything.

The fact that PT boats could afford to dispose of obsolete torpedoes in this fashion was an indication of the way the war was going. The Allies were on the march in increased strength everywhere, and all forces—land, sea, and air—were preparing for the greatest invasion attempt in history, the D day landing on Normandy. This was to be a dagger thrust at the heart of Hitler's Reich, and the PT's were to be at the very point of it.

•

The English Channel is a comparatively small body of water—small enough to be swum—but perhaps more men have died trying to cross it in wartime than any other place in the world. The great Spanish Armada was wrecked there by storms and the guns of Drake. Napoleon's invasion force was stalled by the Channel, and there has long been an unconfirmed rumor (the details of which are still secret to this day) that during World War II the Germans attempted a barge invasion of England but were turned back when the British dumped tons of oil into the sea and set it ablaze.

Invasion forces going the other way—from England to France—have usually had more luck. In World War I millions of men crossed the Channel to fight in France. Now, in June of 1944, the greatest single invasion force in history was poised in England, waiting for the signal that would send it across the Channel.

More than a million men and thousands of ships had been assembled at staging areas along the coast. They included every PT boat that could be spared from other duties.

The Channel was not new to the PT's. They had been operating there for many months, engaged in carrying secret agents across to the French coast. Many agents were dropped into France by parachute, but many more were brought across by PT's, which could make the quick run in an hour or less. All this, of course, was in preparation for the invasion, for no smallest detail could be overlooked and it was vital to have every last scrap of information regarding the enemy's preparations.

In the months before the invasion, during the winter of 1943-44, the boats of Squadron 2, based in England, made nineteen missions for the OSS. This was hazardous work —passing German convoy lanes and minefields to anchor less than 500 yards off beaches dominated by German shore batteries.

Without a sound, engines muffled, crews not speaking above a whisper, the PT's slipped in toward the beach. There was the sighing of the night wind, the rumble of surf, the occasional brief flicker of a match as a German sentry paused to light a cigarette. Somewhere in that darkness ahead was all the might of the Nazi army and its immense fortifications. At any moment the torpedo boat might be spotted. Closer and closer came the beach with its line of white foam. A thousand yards, eight hundred, five hundred. Still no sound.

The skipper gives a whispered order and the engines are secured. The boat is dead in the water now. If anything goes wrong, they will be sitting ducks. Quickly a rubber boat is lowered over the side. The man who is to ride it nods once to the skipper and then drops down into the raft. His equipment is lowered after him. Soundlessly he picks up his oars, casts off, and disappears into the darkness. No one knows his name or his mission. The PT men who carried agents to France in the months before the invasion soon learned not to ask questions.

Now the engines are turned over. The skipper transmits his signals to the engine room, and slowly, looking for all the world like a great black shark, the sharp-nosed boat begins to edge out toward the open sea. For once the PT's are not looking for the enemy. If they see him, they will avoid him. On these secret missions they are under orders to avoid combat whenever possible. In a day, a week, a month, they may return for the nameless man they put ashore. Perhaps he will be there, perhaps not.

By the first week in June, the best and worst kept secret in the world was that the invasion would take place any day. Although every man connected with the plan was sworn to secrecy, it must have been perfectly apparent to the German scout planes and to their agents ashore that the great accumulation of men and ships in the channel ports had only one purpose—imminent invasion. Two long years of planning and effort had gone into the preparations—billions of dollars' worth of war materials had been transported three thousand miles across the ocean; the lives of thousands of men and the freedom of half the world were at stake. All this mighty weight of arms now waited for the decision of General Dwight D. Eisenhower. Never before had any man known quite so awesome a responsibility.

And now, suddenly, there was another element to be reckoned with. The weather. D day had originally been scheduled for daybreak, June 5. Presumably this would be a time—with the fearsome winter gales long gone—of good weather in the Channel. In actual fact it went just the other way. The weather was steadily worsening and the Channel would soon be wracked by the worst gales in forty years. It was bad weather for all concerned, and especially so for small, high-speed craft such as the PT's.

As the rain swept down over the massed fleet and poised armies, as the wind howled among the smokestacks and through the rigging of the ships, some old hands said it would soon clear. Others shook their heads and said there had never been anything like it. Still others said the whole thing would have to be called off. Meanwhile the icy rains swept down on both armies—the Germans behind their Atlantic Wall, and the Allies on board their ships, waiting for the signal.

During those first four days of June, there were almost constant weather conferences. Everyone waited for the Supreme Commander to make up his mind, while he waited for the last word from the weatherman. For the troops huddled in the musty holds of the landing craft, the suspense was almost unbearable, and even the men on the PT's in the gale-torn harbors of Portland and Portsmouth were beginning to show the strain.

The hours dragged by with no further word. Before dawn, on the morning of June 4, the skippers of Squadron 34 waited with idling motors. When no word of cancellation came, they ordered lines let go and proceeded out into the turbulent Channel. They were halfway across to France before they received word that the invasion had been postponed until June 6. PT's very nearly had the dubious honor of invading France a full day before the rest of the Allied forces.

At midnight of the fifth of June, General Eisenhower was still conferring with his meteorologist. The latest prediction at that time was for west to northwest winds slowly moderating. At 4:15 in the morning the General made his final decision and word was passed throughout the fleet.

On board the PT's, men grinned at each other and called out, "Let's go, mate. We've got a date with Hitler." And so this time, with no mistake about it, the invasion was on, and the PT's, with all guns ready, sailed for France.

As the men on the beachheads were battling their way inland past the pillboxes and through the hedgerows of Normandy, the PT's were struggling against rising seas and the constant threat of minefields and E boats. An arbitrary line known as the Mason Line had been established from the beachhead for a distance of six miles out to sea, and the PT's were now called upon to patrol this inner defense perimeter.

It was vital work, for if the German E boats could pierce the Mason Line they would be free to attack the thousands of tons of Allied shipping loading and unloading along the coast.

Day after day, in the teeth of forty-mile gales and mountainous seas, the PT's kept to their patrol stations. Before this, it would have been considered impossible for small wooden fighting ships the size of PT's to function under such conditions. The PT's proved their ability to "take it" far beyond the expectation of the high-ranking officers who had ordered them into position. Some of the boats were in the Mason Line for as long as three weeks without relief—a fantastic ordeal for hulls, engines, and crews.

The Germans, in anticipation of the invasion effort, had dropped thousands of floating mines along the coast, and on the night of June 7, while patrolling near St. Marcouf Island, the PT 505 was wracked by a violent explosion that tore off her stern. Once again the PT's proved their amazing ability to absorb punishment and still remain afloat. At a quick order from the skipper, the 505's watertight compartment doors were dogged shut and an assessment of the damage was made. The explosion had wounded two men, torn loose depth charges, snapped the warheads off torpedoes, and wrenched the engines loose from their moorings. But, although the afterdeck was awash, the 505 was still afloat and her men were determined to save her.

Everything that could be moved was carried forward to

The first of the 70-footers, from which the Elco 80-footer of World War II fame was developed

PT's tied up to finger piers on Woendi Island, Dutch New Guinea

PT's moored under camouflage nets in New Guinea

Papuan scouts on board a PT off the coast of New Guinea

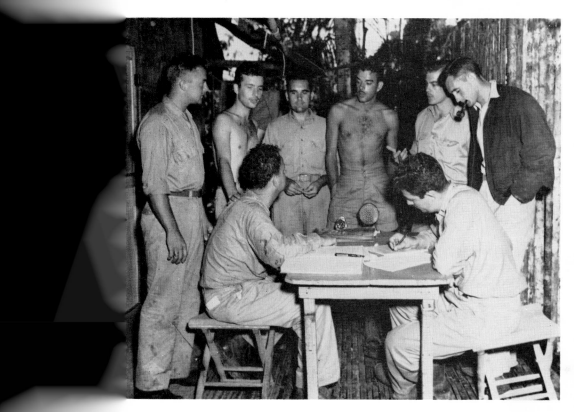

PT skippers in Morobe, New Guinea, report to intelligence officers
after a patrol

A PT gunner searches the sea and sky

PT sailors in the Solomons are reminded of the fighting words of John Paul Jones

Japanese aircraft bombing shipping in Leyte Gulf during the American invasion of November 14, 1944. PT gunners are manning their anti-aircraft weapons

All that was left of the PT 320 after it received a direct bomb hit in Leyte Gulf on November 5, 1944

A PT traveling at high speed fires its two forward torpedoes at the same moment

Oil-smeared Japanese survivors are hauled out of the water after their ship has been sunk by torpedo attack during the Battle of Surigao Strait

During the invasion of Kiska, PT's used these mock figures to disguise the boats as landing barges

A PT gunner on patrol off the black coast of New Guinea prepares for
action with his twin .50 caliber machine guns

A PT mascot takes to his life jacket at Leyte,
Philippine Islands

President Harry Truman giving the Medal of Honor to Lt. Commander
Murray Preston, one of the outstanding PT heroes of the war

A 31-foot PBR, today's modern fiber-glass baby brother to the PT, charges up a river in Vietnam

balance the load, and a signal for help was transmitted to the nearest PT, the 507.

The damaged boat was towed in to the beach through the smashing surf and set ashore. It might reasonably have been supposed that she would be abandoned there, but the men of the 505 had other plans. Despite the fact that they were in the middle of the greatest invasion in history and that all around them was the thunder of big guns and the roar of planes, they set about the job of effecting jury-rig repairs.

In the morning, with the boat now left high and dry by the receding tide, they attached wooden patches to the damaged hull and then waited for the tide to return. One of the crew members seized a paintbrush and scrawled along the side in huge dripping letters: ENGLAND OR BUST.

Inch by inch as the tide rolled in they waited to see if she would refloat herself. The stern lifted, the patches held, the 505 would go to sea again.

Another PT stood in through the surf and cast them a line. To the astonishment of the Germans ashore and the massed landing craft along the beaches, the 505 began to move slowly out away from the coast. Her ordeal, however, was not yet over. Four times during that wretched crossing of the Channel against brutal seas, the towline parted, and each time it seemed as though the 505 might founder. Yet on they went until at last the coastline of England was in sight and the 505 slipped in through the harbor defenses and was home. She was later repaired and lived to fight again.

Meanwhile, the mines were taking a heavy toll of the larger ships. On the morning of the eighth, the destroyer escort *Rich* was torn apart by two mines. Three PT's made fast alongside and refused to leave despite the danger of further explosions. The *Rich*'s decks were awash but the transfer of the wounded went on. As gently as possible, the burned and wounded men of the *Rich* were transferred to the PT's. Some of the PT boatmen were still on board the destroyer when she went down. They were later picked up by another vessel. In all, sixty-nine badly wounded men had been rescued from the sinking *Rich* and taken to safety by the PT's.

Another curious task for the PT's operating off the French coast might have been called Operation Sitting Duck. In the last week of June, as the Germans retreated before the advancing Allied troops, a task force of American battleships and cruisers turned their big guns on the French port of Cherbourg, hoping to knock out its coastal defenses. For more than three hours they pounded away with everything in their arsenals, at the end of which time there was silence from the enemy shore batteries. However, there was no way of knowing if the guns had really been knocked out or if this silence was a trap to lure one of the big ships within range.

It was finally decided that if it were a trap it would have to be sprung. The smallest and most expendable target that could be offered the German gunners was a PT boat. Two PT's approached the harbor and for twenty-five minutes maneuvered back and forth like pleasure boaters out for a Sunday afternoon cruise. At times they were no more than 150 yards off the scowling fortress. There was no sound from the shore, no sign of the enemy.

Had the Germans been able to hold out just a few minutes longer, the admiral commanding the American fleet might have decided that it was safe to send his big ships through the narrow entrance into the harbor, but the sight of those two insolent little boats tail-wagging back and forth in front of them was too much for the Nazi gunners. There was a great boom from the shore and a large-caliber shell burst ahead of the lead boat. Another fell astern of the second PT. For a moment both boats were wreathed in smoke and both were jarred by the impact of the explosions. The 521 boat lay dead in the water, with stalled engines and one torpedo knocked halfway out of its rack. The other PT, dodging the German shell bursts, circled the 521, covering it with a screen of smoke.

Aboard the 521 the engineers worked furiously to start her engines. Within five minutes they were on their way again, heading, as the PT boaters used to say, "for the barn." It was, perhaps, the longest five minutes the men of the 521 would ever know, and while it did resolve the question of whether or not the Germans were still in Cherbourg, it was unanimously concluded on board the 521 that in the future there must be an easier way of finding out.

Unhappily, the good luck the boats had experienced at Cherbourg ran out a few weeks later in the Channel near the Island of Jersey. On the night of August 8, the 509 boat disappeared forever. The 509, in company with other PT's and a United States destroyer, was patrolling through heavy fog to the west of one of the Channel Islands—the Island of Jersey. All afternoon thick yellow banks of fog had been rolling in until at dusk visibility was down to less than a hundred yards. Operating by radar, the boats were moving slowly along a north-south line six miles long, when suddenly the destroyer picked up a flotilla of enemy mine sweepers and ordered the PT's to attack.

It must have been weird, knowing the enemy was just a

few hundred yards ahead in the fog but still invisible. Guided only by the glowworm sweep hand of the radar, the 509 fired a torpedo into the darkness but it missed. The 509 kept closing the range until she passed through an opening in the fog and there were the enemy ships dead ahead. At once there came the crash of gunfire reverberating through the fog. The 509 was between the enemy and the other PT's, which prevented them from opening fire immediately for fear of hitting their own comrades. By the time they could complete their sweep and close in on the enemy, the 509 had vanished. The remaining PT's at once opened fire and a brisk gun duel ensued before the fog rolled in again and the action was broken off.

Two days later the body of one of the men of the 509 was found floating in the Channel along with pieces of wreckage. It was assumed that the 509 had gone down with all hands and that the story of what had happened to her would never be known. But many months later, when the war in Europe had ended and Allied prisoners of war were being released from camps on the Channel Islands, it was learned that the radarman of the 509 had survived and had been taken prisoner on board one of the enemy minesweepers.

The radarman—John L. Page—had been in the charthouse at the time the action opened and could not give a very clear account of what had happened. He had heard the PT's guns banging away at the enemy and then a shell from the minesweeper exploded directly inside the charthouse, wounding Page and killing everyone else.

When Page recovered consciousness, he found his clothing on fire and the whole forward part of the boat in flames. Apparently the dying skipper of the PT had held straight on for his target and the PT had crashed into the side of the minesweeper and was stuck fast there. The Germans were pouring an inferno of small-arms fire and hand grenades down into the wrecked PT. Page was wounded again and again but somehow managed to struggle to the side of the boat and throw himself into the water. Fully expecting to die there, he lay almost senseless in the water. Then someone on the minesweeper threw him a line. He seized it and was pulled aboard.

The last thing he remembered before losing consciousness again was the Germans working desperately to free the flaming wreckage of the PT from the side of their ship. As he was carried below decks, he heard a mighty roar: the PT exploding.

Although Page had been wounded in thirty-seven different places and his right arm and leg had been broken, he survived. There were fifteen dead on the German minesweeper.

After the explosion, the wreckage of the 509 slipped away from the enemy ship down into the black and icy waters of the Channel. It was a gallant end for a PT that even in death had still managed to lash out at the enemy.

•

The disappearance of the 509 boat marked the end of major PT action in the European theater. The hard-pressed enemy was now retreating inland and there was no longer any German coastal traffic to speak of. Some of the PT squadrons were recalled to New York to be re-outfitted for duty in the Pacific. Others sailed to Scotland to be transferred to Russia under Lend Lease.

No history of the PT's in World War II is complete, however, without the story of two squadrons that fought what was perhaps the worst enemy of all, without firing a shot.

Early in 1943 the Japanese fleet in the north Pacific was still a threat to Alaska and to installations in the Aleutian Islands, which curve south and west away from the mainland. Since the bulk of the United States Navy was then heavily engaged in the south and central Pacific, it was decided to send two squadrons of PT's to Alaska to assist in the defense of the Aleutians.

It seems likely in retrospect that whoever made that decision in 1943 did not know very much about PT's. Sending these small, fragile, high-speed boats to operate in such waters was a little like ordering a man to ride across the Antarctic ice to the South Pole on a motorcycle.

The Aleutians—a string of small, rocky, uninhabited islands—are famous for only one thing, the worst weather in the world. The days of sunshine in the course of a year in the Aleutians can be counted on one hand. The prevailing conditions include fog, ice, snow, and sudden fierce storms known as "williwaws." During a williwaw, winds would often get up to 100 miles an hour, and immense, icy seas would batter to death any small craft caught in their grip.

The PT tour of duty in the Aleutians became an endurance contest for men and boats. The boats had no heat except for the warmth given off by their engines and a tiny two-burner galley stove. It was not uncommon to find the inside planking covered with a thick layer of frost, while the decks were weighted down with tons of ice often as much as four inches thick. Simply to survive under such conditions, let alone be ready to fight an enemy who might appear at any moment out of the fog and snow, called for the utmost heroism on the part of the PT crews.

Every man who rode the boats in that grim winter of 1943-44 risked his life every moment he was at sea. Booted feet slid helplessly on icy decks, and fingers froze fast to machine-gun triggers. An exposed ear or nose meant instant frostbite and helmsmen found it almost impossible to handle boats so overloaded with ice.

PT's dragged their anchors in the great squalls and were hurled ashore into snowbanks or onto the ice. Men on watch could hardly move their limbs after only a few minutes of exposure. Spray froze on decks and lifelines. And a single misstep meant instant death in the icy sea.

Day after day, operating from their base at Adak, the PT's struggled against the icy gales, searching for an enemy who never came. Perhaps the Japanese were too busy in the Solomons and New Guinea to spare the ships necessary for a campaign in the Aleutians, or perhaps, after experiencing the ice, fog, snow, and 100-mile-an-hour winds, they decided that it was an area of the world they would gladly leave to the Americans.

8

With the war in Europe drawing to a close, the Navy could now devote its full attention to the still dangerous Japanese. Slowly, island by island, the fight went on. Although it was now quite apparent that the Japanese could no longer win, they were not yet reconciled to losing. They struggled to retain each island, each bloody beachhead first pounded by the Navy and then seized by the Marines. But despite the fanatic resistance of the enemy, the Allied forces continued to push northward, toward the Philippines and eventually toward the islands of Japan.

It was no longer considered necessary to defeat the Imperial Army in New Guinea. With our bases secured there and with Rabaul immobilized, a simpler and more effective strategy presented itself—General MacArthur's concept of the Leapfrog. The PT's had cut off the enemy from his supplies and starved him into near submission and the time had come to leap forward around his flank toward what was to be the last great naval battle of the Pacific—the struggle for the Philippines.

With this in mind, a task force under the command of Rear Admiral Barbey landed on September 15, 1944, on the island of Morotai, about halfway between the northwest tip of New Guinea and the southernmost island of the Philippines. Only twelve miles away across the water was the huge, jungle island of Halmahera, containing a well-equipped Japanese army of nearly 50,000 men. Between this major Japanese force and our men on Morotai stood the PT's.

Long gone were the days when the PT's had been a handful of badly equipped, ramshackle boats. These were new squadrons operating in great strength and with the very latest type of radar to guide them along the Black Coast.

Twenty-four hours after the Army had established a beachhead on Morotai, a force of forty-one new, modern PT's arrived. On the night of September 16, the PT's made their first patrol through the straits between Halmahera and Morotai. These place names were to be engraved on the minds of the PT men, for they were to patrol these waters for the better part of a year, rendering impotent the huge Japanese army that was only twelve miles away.

As with all the islands of the southwest Pacific, the enemy consisted not only of the Japanese but also of the razor-sharp, uncharted coral reefs. Within the first weeks of operations, two PT's had been lost on the reefs and a third boat, the 363, had been destroyed by enemy fire.

The 363 was lost in an unusual action in that it took

place in daylight. On the morning of November 25, the 363 and 362 were returning from a night-long patrol when the lookouts spotted an enemy barge on the beach of Halmahera. This beached barge was part of an enemy trap, but the PT skippers had no way of knowing it at the time.

The two boats came in for a fast run on the barge before turning for home, and at that moment a heavy barrage of machine-gun fire opened from the shore. The 363 was hit in the engine room and stopped dead in the water. By radio the skipper of the 363 notified the 362 that he was under heavy fire and was unable to proceed. The skipper of the 362 placed his boat between the 363 and the beach to draw the enemy fire. The 362 made two high-speed runs with every gun blasting away at the shore batteries, but midway of the second run she was hit amidships by an enemy shell. Although the 362 was still able to navigate, she was in a bad way, and at last she turned back to the 363 to try to tow her out of danger.

By this time heavy shells from the enemy three-inch guns had been added to the hail of machine-gun bullets. Both boats were now being struck repeatedly, and Lieutenant Mitchell, the skipper of the 363, had been mortally wounded. It was obvious that there was no longer any hope of saving the 363 and the best that could be done would be to attempt to save her crew.

Despite the heavy fire from the beach, the 362 stood by and began the transfer of wounded from the other PT. This operation had to be carried out under the most difficult conditions, with only one gun on the 362 still able to return the enemy's fire.

At last the transfer was complete and the bullet-riddled 362 managed to pull away, leaving the sinking 363 behind.

Twenty-six men had been wounded, and Lieutenant Mitchell had been killed. It was a heartbreaking experience for the squadrons at Morotai and it brought home a bitter lesson that had been learned in the early days but now had to be relearned in this painful way—that PT's were far too vulnerable to operate in daylight. They were hunters of the night and the Black Coast was their natural habitat.

As if in revenge for the loss of the 363, the PT's at Morotai began a determined drive against the enemy's coastal shipping. In the following eleven months they made 1,300 patrols and destroyed fifty barges and almost 200 other Japanese small craft. Despite these setbacks, the Japanese were still making efforts to reinforce their garrison on Morotai, but the hornets' nest of PT's stung them so repeatedly that they were never able to cross the twelve-mile strait between the two islands.

In addition to cutting off the barge traffic, the PT's were ranging far afield on scouting missions. One of the most interesting of these special patrols took place during the first week in April. Native scouts came out of the jungles of the island of Hiri with the report that a sultan there was ready to leave the island and join the Allies. Two boats, carrying a rescue team of Australian soldiers and native scouts, were sent in to pick up the sultan. The operation went off without a hitch, except that the skippers of the PT's were surprised to find that picking up the Sultan meant picking up his considerable number of wives as well. Thus, for a short time, the two PT's constituted a sort of seagoing harem.

This was not the last time that PT's were used to transport family groups. Toward the end of the war, in September 1945, a force of PT's evacuated several hundred internees, most of them women and children, from a camp at Kuching, Borneo. At one point in the New Guinea campaign a group of missionaries and nuns were evacuated by PT's from an area behind the Japanese lines. From the early days of the war, when the PT's had first evacuated General MacArthur and his family from the Philippines, they had in a sense come full circle.

While the purpose of the nightly PT patrols out of Morotai was still largely the containment of the great Japanese force on Halmahera, there were now added an increasing number of highly secret scouting missions. One of the strangest of these was the destruction of the formidable "South Seas Development Company," a Japanese civilian trading firm with warehouses and offices on Halmahera and the offshore islands.

Although ostensibly civilian, the main function of the South Seas Development Company in those days was to provide food for the hard-pressed Japanese army on Halmahera. Food was stolen from the natives and stored in the company's warehouses until it could be moved to the army by native outrigger canoes. Many of these canoes were quite large, being shaped like sailing prahus thirty to forty feet long, and were capable of transporting a ton or more of food at a time. Since this heavy traffic was conducted, ostensibly, by the natives themselves, it was determined that the only way to break it up would be by means of PT's.

On the morning of July 5, Lieutenant Joe Burk, one of the outstanding skippers of the New Guinea campaign, led two PT's carrying thirty-seven native scouts on a raid that was to prove the beginning of the end for the South Seas Development Company.

Close in to Makian Island they spotted two heavily laden prahus and rapidly overtook them. After a swift conversation between the scouts and the natives in the prahus, it was learned that these supplies were on their way to the Japanese. Burk ordered the natives taken aboard the PT's and the prahus sunk. The boats then proceeded in to the company dock at Makian Island and set fire to all warehouses and the headquarters building. Leaving the company buildings blazing behind them, the boats then destroyed eight more prahus they found along the beach.

The PT's struck again a few days later. Carrying extra fuel tanks, they ranged as far as 200 miles from their base at Morotai and left behind them a trail of blazing warehouses, frightened natives, and ruined prahus. Destruction is never a pretty thing, but it is an essential element of warfare, and in their first try at it, the PT's turned out to be masters of the art. Warehouses, sago mills, radio stations, and canoes were all set afire. Soon trails of black smoke darkened the air above the islands surrounding Halmahera.

So swiftly were the PT's moving that the Japanese had no time or opportunity to fight back. In only one case was resistance encountered. A force of six enemy soldiers opened fire with machine guns on a landing party. However, a salvo of shells from the PT's 37 mm. cannon soon silenced them and sent them to meet their ancestors.

By the end of the month, after repeated raids, it was clear that the South Seas Development Company had gone out of business. The remaining warehouses and supply depots had been abandoned and the army on Halmahera was left to fend for itself. Thus the PT's had the unique distinction of emerging victorious in the only battle of its kind in history—an engagement between a seagoing naval force and a land-based commercial enterprise.

But, farcical as this skirmish with the South Seas Development Company may have been, it was clearly only preparation for greater things to come. At that moment—in Tokyo and Yokohama, in Washington and at Pearl Harbor —the admirals and the generals were burning the lights long after dark, conferring on what was to be the next great step of the southwest Pacific war—the return to the Philippines.

It had now been three and a half years since the PT's of Squadron 3 had taken General MacArthur out of the Philippines and had heard him promise, "I shall return." Now the tremendous power of the Allied forces was poised for what was as great a gamble in the Pacific as D day had been in the European theater. And the PT's, which had been the last to leave the Philippines, were to be among the first to return.

A vast accumulation of naval strength—the greatest the world had ever seen—was poised for the thrust. So enormous was this force that it operated under four separate commands, each of which was basically responsible only to the President of the United States. The Japanese in turn had mustered three separate fleets, the last of their once great strength—in order to repel the invasion. It was a battle such as the world had never seen before and is unlikely ever to see again. And the PT's—tiny wooden arrows among all these behemoths—were the first craft to be launched against the enemy.

THE PHILIPPINE ISLANDS

9

To comprehend fully the Battle of Leyte, one must first understand the composition of the forces that were involved.

The greatest naval engagement in history had been the tremendous Battle of Jutland in World War I, in which 151 British ships fought to the death against ninety-nine German ships. It was a costly battle for the British, but it resulted in the virtual end of the German fleet as an effective force and was considered a victory. Much the same pattern was to be repeated at Leyte, but on an even larger scale, for 216 American ships, including 39 PT's, engaged 64 Japanese ships. But the size of the battle cannot be judged by ships alone. Thousands of aircraft were also involved. (There were no aircraft at all in the Battle of Jutland.) More than 143,000 American officers and enlisted men fought in the battle for Leyte, which was more than the entire strength of the United States Navy and Marine Corps had been before World War II.

Although the Japanese had been in general retreat across the Pacific for a year, they were far from beaten. They had in fact been saving their most powerful ships for the last and greatest battle. Among these were the world's largest fighting ships—the incredibly powerful new battleships *Yamato* and *Musashi*—each completed in 1942 and each displacing more than 68,000 tons. These were the so-called "mystery ships" of the Japanese Navy, of which the world had been hearing rumors for some years. Not only were these ships far bigger than any in the American Navy, but also they carried heavier guns—18-inch cannon, as against our 16-inchers—and were capable of fantastic speeds of 27 knots—almost the speed of the PT's. Although on occasion these monster battleships had been seen briefly (the *Yamato* had taken part in the Battle of Midway), the Japanese had obviously been saving them for the greatest battle of all and they were now aimed directly toward the Philippines.

Not content with this enormous sea force which was now steaming toward Leyte, the Japanese admirals ordered more than 800 land-based planes sent from Japan and China. This was to compensate for the tremendous number of Japanese carrier planes lost in the earlier battle of the Philippine Sea.

Out of this shortage of carrier planes grew the famous kamikaze tactics. The term *kamikaze* means "heavenly wind" and it comes from a well-known episode in Japanese history. In the year 1570 the Mongols were preparing for an invasion of Japan and had assembled a great fleet on the coast of China. Before the invasion fleet reached Japan, however, it was destroyed by a typhoon which was supposedly a heavenly wind sent by the gods to protect Japan. The name kamikaze was now applied to suicide pilots who were ordered to crash their bomb-laden planes directly onto the decks of the Allied ships. It was a last-ditch maneuver that, like the Battle of Leyte, came close to succeeding.

The Japanese plan—known as the SHO-1 plan—was highly ingenious. The key to it involved a decoy force which, it was hoped, would draw off the powerful American Third Fleet and leave the way open for the Japanese battleships and cruisers to smash the transports unloading on the beach. If the plan were successful, it would destroy the greatest invasion force the Allies had been able to muster in the Pacific and would certainly prolong the war by many years. The Japanese strategy was by that time based on the hope not of winning the war but of stalemating it.

The battle for Leyte was to comprise every type of naval warfare ever invented: gunfire of heavy and light ships, bombing, kamikazes, strafing, rocketing and torpedoing by aircraft, submarines, destroyers and motor-torpedo boats. The Japanese had been preparing for many months. The actual moment of attack was to be known as "X day," meaning execution day for the American forces who would be establishing the Philippine beachhead.

It was a desperate gamble for the Japanese—the same sort of gamble the Germans took with the remnants of their once great Panzer tank forces during the Battle of the Bulge—for if it failed it would mean the end of the Japanese Navy as a striking force.

This then was the situation in the fall of 1944—the PT's

were about to be thrown headlong into the greatest naval battle of all. The stage was set and the actors were beginning to move onto the scene.

By the first week in September, Admiral Halsey's powerful Third Fleet was sweeping ever closer to the Philippines. American carrier planes were pounding shore installations on Mindanao and had downed almost two hundred enemy planes. Japanese resistance appeared to be weakening, and Halsey therefore proposed to Admiral Nimitz that the invasion of the Philippines take place ahead of schedule.

It had been originally thought that the first landings would take place on Mindanao, but with Japanese resistance crumbling, it was decided to bypass Mindanao and go straight to Leyte, in the very heart of the Philippines. Once this decision was taken, enormous forces were set in motion on both sides.

On October 17, the first American troops were landed on two small islands guarding the approaches to Leyte Gulf. The PT's had not waited for the actual landings to take place. By October 13, they were already on their way to the Philippines, for they had a long way to go. They would have to travel 1,200 miles from their base in New Guinea to reach Leyte. After several different plans for transporting them had been abandoned for tactical reasons, it was finally decided to let the boats make the trip under their own power. Tenders accompanied the PT's to refuel them at sea, and it took the forty-five PT's a little over a week to make the long sea voyage, the largest and longest mass operation ever attempted by PT's.

The PT's went into action immediately after their arrival, sinking several barges that first night. But this brisk exchange of gunfire was only a preliminary for the tremen-

106

dous events that were to take place. Although a pall of muggy heat hung heavily over the jungle and the beaches, and there was still no sign of real resistance on the part of the enemy, an air of expectancy seemed to charge the atmosphere around the boats. No one really believed the Japanese would relinquish the Philippines without a struggle. Their fleet must be on its way. But where was it and when would it strike?

On the afternoon of October 24, the PT squadrons received the word they had been waiting for. They were to proceed south at full speed to patrol the entrance to Surigao Strait. It was through this strait that the Japanese fleet must come if they were to attack. Sending all PT's out on patrol meant that the enemy was on his way and the PT's would be first in line to intercept him. Behind the PT's were the destroyers, and behind them the cruisers and battleships. That night the PT's would be the eyes of the fleet, the first American ships the Japanese would encounter as they steamed toward Leyte.

The motors turned over, and boat after boat backed away from its berth and sped south at full speed. Bows high, long wakes streaming, flags whipping in the wind, the boats were an impressive sight as they charged toward the mouth of the Strait. Never before had so many PT's been assembled for a single mission; never before had they been on a mission so important.

Guns were cleared—the flat chatter of the "fifties" and the heavy thump of the "forties" sounding out across the bay—and then the PT's settled down for the night's work.

After countless gun battles with small craft, this, at last, was what they had been waiting for—a chance to use their torpedoes against capital ships. It was what they had been built for and what they had been waiting for all during the war.

Weather conditions in the Strait that night were perfect. The sea was calm, almost glassy smooth, and when the quartering moon set shortly after midnight the sky went inky black. Motors turning over slowly, gun crews at their positions, the boats lay on their assigned stations—waiting.

Steaming toward them—only a few miles away now—was Vice Admiral Nishimura and his powerful task force of battleships, cruisers, and destroyers. The moon had set. Out of the blackness came the Japanese. Toward them charged the PT's.

We cannot know what was passing through Admiral Nishimura's mind that night as he led his task force into the narrow mouth of Surigao Strait, but we can suppose that he felt confident.

The SHO-1 battle plan had begun with an initial success. Admiral Halsey had accepted the bait and had gone steaming off to the north on a wild-goose chase after the Japanese Northern Force. Sixty-five of the American Navy's newest and most powerful ships and the great bulk of its carrier planes were off chasing seventeen Japanese ships that had been deliberately arranged as a decoy. The only force the Japanese had really feared had been the Third Fleet and now the Third Fleet could no longer be considered an active threat.

SHO-1 was already functioning, and the second act of the drama was about to unfold. There was no reason to suppose it would not go as smoothly. With Halsey out of the way, it would be relatively easy for the Japanese Center Force under Admiral Kurita and the Southern Force under Nishimura to meet at Leyte, approaching from different directions and squeezing the Americans between them. By the time Halsey became aware of the trick that had been played on him, the damage would be done; the American forces at Leyte would no longer exist.

It was true that the American Seventh Fleet under Admiral Kinkaid still had considerable fire power in its battleships, but it was equally true that these were old ships, resurrected from the mud at Pearl Harbor and antiquated even before the start of the war. Certainly they were no match for the *Yamato* and the *Musashi,* the two mightiest warships in the world.

No one could have known that Nishimura would die that night and with him his entire fleet. Out of the hundreds of thousands of tons of steel now steaming into the mouth of Surigao Strait, only one Japanese ship would still be afloat when the action was over.

•

Two hours before midnight, four PT's under the tactical command of Lieutenant Pullen, a veteran of the New Guinea campaign, were eighteen miles off the coast of Bohol. The PT's radar had given warning of the approach of enemy ships, but their size and number could not be calculated. Lookouts on the PT's were straining their eyes into the blackness and now they saw in the last glimmer of moonlight immense shapes of battleships and heavy cruisers moving swiftly and smoothly toward them.

Almost immediately, with the PT's still out of torpedo firing range, the enemy ships opened fire. Great red flowers blossomed suddenly all along the silhouette of Japanese ships. Star shells arced across the sky and the PT's found themselves pinned in the hard blue light. As always, the

Japanese ships had excellent gunners. That first salvo, fired at a range of more than three miles, bracketed the PT's and the 130 boat received a direct hit from an eight-inch gun. Once again the miraculous good luck of the PT's came into play. An eight-inch shell should have reduced the PT to a mass of splinters and a puddle of oil, but the shell landed on the 130's forward-port torpedo, smashing the warhead and ripping up the deck planking. After striking the torpedo, the shell passed through the hull above the waterline and emerged on the other side. Neither the torpedo nor the shell exploded, and no one on board received so much as a scratch. "Somebody up there" was most certainly watching over the 130 boat that night.

Unable to close the range, the PT's retired behind a smoke screen with the Japanese destroyers in hot pursuit. The 152 boat was struck by a 4.7-inch shell and did not share in the 130's luck. The gunner on the PT's 37 mm. gun was fatally wounded and the boat was set afire.

The 152 boat, however, was far from finished. She dropped two depth charges and turned to face the massive adversary bearing down on her. The destroyer's bow wave was creaming in the moonlight and the great steel prow was almost on top of her when the charges exploded and the destroyer was forced to turn away. Not content with having routed the destroyer, Lieutenant Pullen tried to close in for an attack on the larger ships, but his damaged boat was unable to make the speed necessary to catch the enemy. The 152 at last, reluctantly, gave up the fight.

The main purpose of sending the PT's into Surigao Strait that night had been to give the first warning of the approach of the enemy. With shells bursting all around them, the PT skippers were now frantically trying to contact Command by radio to relay their information, but so intense was the concussion from bursting shells that they were unable to make their radios work. More than two hours passed before the PT's could establish radio contact, and during that time all the boats were engaged with the enemy.

The battle was now beginning to spread all across the mouth of the Strait. PT's found themselves struggling for their lives against the immense black forms that seemed to be arriving in ever increasing numbers. The moonlight played strange tricks, shining bright one moment and obscured the next by sudden rain squalls. Big as the Japanese ships were, they were made to appear even bigger in the moonlight and their sudden disappearance in the squalls lent the entire scene a ghostly, nightmarish quality.

A considerable distance northeast of Lieutenant Pullen's group, another section of PT's under Lieutenant Owen was also engaged. Although Owen and his group knew the enemy was coming, they had no way of estimating his strength. All efforts at establishing radio contact with Pullen's group had failed. Now, across the horizon to the south, they saw a spreading array of gun flashes, searchlights, and starshells. Suddenly a squall blotted everything from view, but then, as the sky cleared and the moon illuminated the water before them, they saw, less than two miles away, the great hulking shape of a battleship flanked by cruisers and destroyers.

As the boats deployed for the attack, they were lit up by searchlights from the enemy ships. Boring in despite the light, they were taken under fire by the battleship. With shells bursting all around them and with a destroyer now close on their heels, they managed to launch two torpedoes before being forced to retreat under cover of smoke. Though still able to operate, the command boat, PT 151, had been riddled by shell fragments, and Owen thought it best to pull his section back behind the smoke in order to wait for another opportunity.

The enemy seemed to be everywhere, and the PT's darted between the great ships. The scene was one of such confusion that it was impossible to know how many of the torpedoes scored hits, but of one at least we can be sure— a torpedo fired by the 137 boat that struck the light cruiser *Abakuma.* Its consequences were so far reaching that it is unquestionably the most important single fish ever fired by a PT boat.

As it turned out, the force they were now encountering was only the first wave of the attackers. Behind Admiral Nishimura's fleet was another powerful force under Admiral Shima. The shock effect of the SHO-1 plan was to be doubled by the arrival of this second force less than thirty miles behind the first. But, as in all such operations, timing was everything. To have the effect planned by the Imperial Command, Shima's force must arrive neither too soon nor too late.

Now, however, Nishimura's fleet found itself delayed by the PT's. As it shrugged off one swarm of the mosquito boats, another group rushed in to sting from the other side. Nishimura could not seem to rid himself of these little plywood devils, nor was there any hope now of achieving a surprise attack. PT reports had been coming in for some time, giving Admiral Kinkaid a clear picture of exactly where the enemy was and in what strength. But, even more important, as Nishimura's fleet milled about, trying to cope with the PT's, Shima's force was steadily closing in behind him. The Japanese timetable was being thrown out of gear by the maddening little boats that kept charging in and out of the smoke at Nishimura's ships.

Thirty-nine PT's were involved in the Battle of Surigao Strait that night, and at least thirty were under enemy fire at various times. Ten were hit. Amazingly enough, only one boat—the 493—struck by three 4-inch shells—was lost. Three PT crewmen were killed, and three officers and seventeen men were wounded. Thirty-five torpedoes were fired, and of these only one—the torpedo that struck the *Abakuma*—was definitely known to be a direct hit.

The 137 boat, under the command of Lieutenant Kovar, had been struggling all through the earlier part of the evening with a faulty radar set, which now had given up the ghost completely. Dependent on the eyes of her lookouts, she was at a pronounced disadvantage in the reduced visibility of the squally night. Therefore she was taken almost entirely by surprise by the enemy ships attempting to pass through the Strait.

Shortly after midnight, Kovar spotted two destroyers proceeding at high speed past his station. He did manage to fire one torpedo in their direction, but he was too far astern to do any good. Sourly he conceded to his second officer that it was simply not his night.

The 137 continued on her patrol, and at 3:30 in the morning Kovar saw another enemy destroyer—this one returning down the Strait. He closed to within 900 yards and fired one torpedo, which was observed to pass beneath the enemy ship. Convinced that he had missed again, Kovar was about to turn away when he heard a loud underwater explosion. Kovar shook his head in bewilderment. Could his fish have struck something after all, or was the explosion due to some other source?

What Kovar could not see in the blackness was another ship beyond the destroyer. She was the cruiser *Abakuma*, and the explosion Kovar had heard was his torpedo striking her.

At once the cruiser fell out of her position, slowing down the entire formation. Nishimura's fleet was once more delayed, and this time fatally, for coming up behind him now was the Japanese second wave under Admiral Shima.

The explosion of the PT's torpedo had killed thirty men on the *Abakuma* and reduced her speed to ten knots. While Nishimura delayed, Admiral Shima's force came charging full tilt into the narrow Strait. With a thunderous crash, Shima's flagship, the *Nachi*, collided with the *Mogami* of Nishimura's force. Perhaps Shima was bewildered by the collision, or perhaps he sensed the impending catastrophe, but whatever the reason, he ordered his badly damaged *Nachi* backed away from the other ship. And then, with the rest of his force about him, Shima fled back into the open water and away from the battle.

Nishimura was now alone, his fleet exposed to the tremendous firepower of Admiral Oldendorf's battleships. These were the old ships *Mississippi, Maryland, West Virginia, Tennessee, California,* and *Pennsylvania,* which had been sunk at Pearl Harbor by the Japanese sneak attack and then raised from the mud. They were now to have all the revenge they could have asked for. The action did not last long and the disorganized Japanese could offer little resistance. When it was over, Nishimura was dead, and all his fleet, with the exception of a single destroyer, had vanished beneath the black waters of Surigao Strait.

10

▼

As if seeking revenge against the PT's that had contributed so mightily to Nishimura's defeat, the Japanese now began a series of concentrated air attacks against the boats operating around the Philippines. Presumably the major purpose of these air strikes was the harassment of all United States shipping in Leyte Gulf, but time and again, in the days that followed the action in Surigao Strait, Japanese planes disregarded other targets in order to swoop down on PT's.

As a measure of their determination, the enemy now began to use kamikaze tactics. The PT's, thanks to their lightning maneuverability, were usually able to avoid these death dives, but on the afternoon of December 10, the 323 boat was struck amidships by a suicide plane and almost totally destroyed. The captain and second officer were killed and eleven men were wounded. At almost the same moment, another plane dived at the PT 532. Like a broken-field runner heading for a touchdown, the skipper of the 532 coolly held his course until the very last moment. When the kamikaze had already begun its dive and was less than 500 yards away, Lieutenant Stephens put the 532 into a hard left turn. Engines howling and propellers almost clear of the water, the 532 spun about and ripped across its own wake as the kamikaze struck the water less than twenty-five yards away. The plane exploded on contact, showering the boat with debris but otherwise doing no damage. All hands agreed that it had been much too close for comfort.

On other occasions the intense PT anti-aircraft fire proved even more effective than the dodging tactics. PT's 195, 522, and 324 each shot down enemy planes in flight. The PT tender *Oyster Bay* was also credited with three planes.

Their luck could not hold indefinitely, however, and on the morning of November 5 a high-flying plane scored an almost incredibly lucky bomb hit on the deck of the 320 boat, which was at anchor at the time. The 320 was totally demolished and had only one survivor.

There were repeated duels between boat skippers and Japanese pilots. On one occasion a "Zeke" fighter came out of the sun in pursuit of the 494 boat and proceeded to turn and twist with every move the PT made. Lieutenant Moran, skipper of the 494, tried every move in the book to make the enemy pilot commit himself, but the Jap held back, coolly waiting for his opportunity. How long this game might have gone on or who might have been the eventual winner will never be known, for at that moment a shell from the PT's 40 mm. cannon tore a piece out of the Zeke's wing and the plane crashed into the water only a few feet astern of the torpedo boat.

But the Japanese were unable to maintain this intensive aircraft activity, for, as the American troops ashore proceeded inland against bitter resistance, the enemy was forced to throw every plane he could muster into the ground battle. Accordingly, the pressure on the PT's patrolling around Leyte and Mindoro began to ease.

If there were fewer planes to fight, there were still plenty of barges and destroyers. Once again the enemy was attempting to supply his forces ashore by the use of luggers and barges, and once again the PT's set out to cut off the enemy's coastal traffic. Night after night, all through December and into March, the PT's were engaged in quick gunfights and smashing torpedo attacks.

One torpedo attack against a destroyer in the Leyte area achieved textbook perfection. Seldom were conditions so ideal, and never before had the goal been achieved so beautifully. On the night of December 11, Lieutenant Haines in the PT 492 spotted a destroyer lying still in the water off the west coast of Leyte. As a rule, Japanese lookouts were far too good to allow a PT to approach within firing range unobserved. But on this occasion Haines was able to work his boat between the destroyer and the beach so as to improve his own visibility and at the same time obscure the PT against the jungle.

Yard by yard the PT crept forward, resisting the strong temptation to come roaring in for a quick strike before it was observed. The only sound was the muted rumble of the exhausts, the gentle swish of water along the hull. It seemed impossible to creep in so close, and at any moment the PT expected the destroyer's guns to burst into flame. But the enemy ship, big and black against the night sky, lay quiet.

At last the PT was only a thousand yards from its target, and still unobserved. It was the sort of situation every PT man dreams of. Easing into position, Haines sighted his target for the last time and gave a quick hand signal to the men standing by the racks. With a splash that was no noisier than a large fish breaking water, the torpedoes dropped over the side and steadied on course straight for the target.

There was a blinding flash directly beneath the destroyer's bridge, and another, a moment later, amidships. The entire ship seemed to explode, sending a fountain of oil, flame, and debris into the air. When the smoke had cleared, the destroyer was gone, the calm black water had closed over her, and the night was as quiet as ever. Clearly, the Japanese never knew what hit them.

On board the PT the men blinked and stared at each other speechlessly for a moment. It had been almost too easy. In the long course of the war, with its thousands of patrols, no PT had ever scored so effortless a victory.

Meanwhile, the nightly gun battles with the barges and luggers went on, with the boats enjoying good hunting all through the winter and into early spring. As the Eighth Army advanced across Leyte, the PT's moved with them, steadily frustrating the enemy's attempt to supply his troops ashore.

One of the strangest engagements—when PT's destroyed not a seagoing craft but a freight train—took place on the evening of March 24. Two PT's, disregarding the enemy's shore defenses, dashed straight into the harbor at

Cebu City and closed to within half a mile of the wharf. A string of freshly loaded freight cars was assembled on the wharf, and, despite the enemy's 75 mm. guns, which were now firing at the PT's, the boats opened fire on the train and set it ablaze before turning their attention to the enemy gunners. So far as is known, this was the first and last engagement fought between a railroad train and a PT boat.

•

The war in the Philippines went on, but it was largely a land war now. The enemy navy never recovered from its tremendous defeat in the battle for Leyte Gulf, and as the spring of 1945 advanced, the targets for PT boats were few and far between.

There were still occasional skirmishes with enemy planes and suicide boats, and now and then a good haul of barges or other small craft, but these were hardly enough to keep all the PT squadrons busy. For the PT's had now grown to a mighty force. Base 17, on the island of Samar, had become the largest and best-equipped PT base in the world, its warehouses filled with millions of dollars' worth of supplies and spare parts. There were now, in mid-1945, 212 PT's operating in the Philippines—a force of more than a thousand officers and ten thousand men. Quite a difference from the day when the last two PT boats had limped out of the Philippines before the advancing Japanese forces.

It was with great satisfaction that the men of the PT's now returned General MacArthur to Corregidor. He had left the Rock in PT 41 on March 11, 1942. Three years later, almost to the day, on March 2, 1945, he came back to Corregidor on board PT 373.

The PT war was almost over, except for one final, tragic incident. The last two PT boats to be destroyed in the war were sunk by error by two American destroyers. The two boats had tried vainly to identify themselves by radio and visual signals, but they were taken under fire by the destroyers. Both boats, the 79 and the 77 were sunk. This problem of faulty recognition, which had pursued the boats through the war, was with them to the end. Both boat captains, who had fought so long and so hard against the enemy, were killed, but thirty survivors of the two boats did manage to make their way ashore and were ultimately rescued by other PT's.

The fighting would still go on, and the PT's would advance all the way to Borneo and to places with exotic names such as Zamboanga, Panay, Tarakan, Tawi Tawi, and Balikpapan, but the great days of the flaming battles against the barges and the dashing torpedo runs against the Japanese battleships were over.

The final battle, for the Japanese home islands, still remained to be fought, and the projected invasion scheme, Operation Olympic, suggested the possible use of two hundred or more PT's. But the enemy surrender came before the actual invasion could be put into effect. The PT squadrons and their weary crews began the long journey homeward.

Many boats, however, did not go home after all. A large number of the fragile hulls had been so badly strained under combat conditions that it would not pay to transport them all the way back across the Pacific to repair facilities in the United States. Furthermore, with the war over, the Navy Department could not see the need for maintaining a large PT fleet in readiness. It was decided, therefore, to destroy the boats where they were. Accordingly 118 PT boats were assembled on the beach at Samar in the Philippines and burned. The remaining boats, those that were considered still serviceable, and new boats that had been placed on order before the end of the war, were put up for sale by the War Shipping Administration. Thus, for a year or two after the war, it was possible to buy, for as little as four or five thousand dollars, a new, or almost new, PT that had cost the government half a million dollars.

Although this was certainly a great bargain, not all the boats were snapped up as readily as one might expect. For one thing, they were warships and would have required considerable expenditure to be converted into yachts. For another, very few yachtsmen could have afforded the almost fantastic amounts of gasoline necessary to run a PT. It was possible, of course, to take out the engine and put in a smaller one that would not burn so much fuel, but then the performance of the boats would be gone. However, some of the boats were converted, and even today you will occasionally see a former PT hull sporting the flying bridge and trunk cabin of a peacetime yacht.

As for the future of the PT: in an age of nuclear warships and Polaris submarines, the future of the PT seems doubtful. Since the end of the war, the Navy has conducted some limited experiments with new and larger PT's, and in 1951 four totally new PT's were accepted by the Navy. These boats were all built of aluminum and averaged some twenty feet longer than the wartime PT's. They carried four engines instead of three, as did the wartime boats, and despite their increased size were still capable of speeds in excess of 40 knots. Perhaps the most interesting aspect of their development is that the PT of the future may not be a motor-torpedo boat at all but a motor-rocket boat. For the rocket, with its high firepower, low recoil, and great accuracy, holds even more promise as a weapon of sea warfare than did the torpedo in its day.

11

Although the PT's are no longer in existence as an active part of the Navy, the lessons learned from their superb performance in World War II have not been forgotten. No other warship can be produced as quickly or as cheaply or serve the same function. The great assets of speed, maneuverability, shallow draft, and high firepower will again make them invaluable, should the need ever arise. And with rockets that can give them the equivalent punch of a World War II light cruiser, they will be a fearsome weapon indeed.

Today there is hardly a high-speed powerboat anywhere that has not benefited in some way from the PT-hull design. And the war in Vietnam, although not primarily a naval war, has produced a surprisingly effective little brother to the PT, the Navy's new patrol craft for policing the winding rivers and channels of the Mekong Delta.

This river patrol boat, known as the PBR, like the PT grew out of very special requirements and, like the PT, was developed largely because of the interest and effort of a civilian rather than a Navy designer.

Early in 1965, the Navy realized that a new kind of Black Coast had come into being—the vast, eerie, silent reaches of the Mekong Delta, where the Vietcong were able to establish supply dumps and bases that are invisible to aircraft. Some type of vessel was needed to patrol these jungle waters. It was thought at first that the need could be filled by the Coast Guard's standard 82-foot cutter. Experience soon showed, however, that the Coast Guard boats were too big for those narrow waters, and their propellers were continually being fouled by weeds and floating logs. It seemed, for a while, as though the Mekong would have to be left to the Vietcong.

Again, as in the case of Mr. Sutphen, who had labored so hard to assist the Navy with the development of the PT before World War II, a private individual came along with the answer to the problem. This time it was Willis Slane, president of the Hatteras Yacht Company. Realizing that what was needed was a small, maneuverable craft that could quietly cruise the shallow waters of the delta and yet be fast enough and carry heavy enough guns to overtake and halt the Vietcong sampans, he produced a thirty-one-foot fiber-glass hull with a most unusual propulsion device. What Slane had in mind was the newly developed water-jet pump that will in time make the propeller as obsolete on boats as the jet engine had made it obsolete on planes.

In boats using the water jet, a pump sucks up water and

then propels it from the stern of the boat with enormous force, thus pushing the boat ahead and doing away with all the vulnerable and expensive underwater parts such as struts, shaft, propeller, and rudder. The boat is steered simply by moving the jet in different directions. Perhaps the greatest advantage of this is that it allows the boat to operate in only a few inches of water.

The Navy quickly saw the favorable aspects of Slane's design, and by using fiber-glass hulls it was able to go into immediate production with great numbers of the PBR's. The Navy's initial order was for a hundred PBR's, with perhaps more coming if the war in Vietnam continues. The boats, despite their small size, pack a considerable punch with their twin .50 caliber machine guns in an armored turret and their single .30 caliber gun set farther aft. In addition, they carry radio, radar, and boarding equipment. They are, in their own way, tiny but quite complete vest-pocket warships. Yet, new as they are (the PBR's are the first naval vessels to employ jet propulsion), one can see in their hull lines a direct heritage from their bigger and older brothers—the PT's of World War II, which fought so gallantly up and down the black coasts on both sides of the world.

INDEX

129